IS AGENDA 2063 FOR ME?

DIASPORA The 6th Region

Empowering Africa and The Diaspora.

For more information, or to book an event, contact :
admin@africanaviationspace.com

Book Editing by David Asomani
Cover design by Josiah Patel

ISBN - Paperback : 9781738462100
ISBN - Hardcover : 9781738462117
ISBN - Kindle : 9781738462124

First Edition: December 2023*

CONTENTS

Chapter 1

Is Agenda 2063 For Me?

IS AGENDA 2063 FOR ME?

Africa reminds me of my grandmother, a woman who for me was the epitome of African strength and love. If you are like me a diaspora and a passionate child of the African continent, or a diaspora who knows little about the continent but yearns to know more, my call is to you. You are an essential part of Africa's story, and a voice for the African continent.

In the pages of this book, I hope to take you on a journey of discovery to understand the broad coverage of the diaspora and the beauty in this 6th region embracing Agenda 2063.

As we embark on a transformative exploration of Africa's future and the significant role you play in it, we will delve into the rich tapestry of Africa's past and the visionary goals of Agenda 2063. I hope to show you how, as a member of the diaspora, you can contribute to the continent's progress through alignment of your passions and skills with the strategic framework of Agenda 2063.

The question this book asks is a pertinent one that I hope you will have extensive clarity on through this book.

Is Agenda 2063 for me? Although the answer to this question is **YES**, the truth is, this is a question that only you have the answer to, because the answer is *"Yes, if you want it to be."*

I hope to provide some insight, inspiration and facts as to why I believe that Agenda 2063 presents a turning point in the story of Africa and is relevant to you today. We will not only look at some personal stories but also look at an overview of Agenda

2063 that will hopefully help you see yourself as part of the implementation of this plan.

There is a tendency for us to stay stuck in the past, but I am excited to share with you the changes that are happening in Africa today as a result of the targeted and strategic actions of Agenda 2063.

There is a generation living within reach of the possibilities and reality of the Africa we want to see, the world we want to see. A generation that understands the beauty and brilliance in diversity, action and most importantly unity.

"I am not African because I was born in Africa
but because Africa was born in me."
-Kwame Nkrumah

This book aims to provide insightful information about Agenda 2063, but more than that it is a call to action. A call to realise your part and maintain a success conscious attitude in your pursuit of it, to let go of the past and walk boldly into a new united future.

This does not mean that we are disregarding the realities of the past, or of life. We are not by this expecting success to come effortlessly. This is about adopting and developing a mindset that empowers the spirit of excellence and motivates us to take strategic and most importantly proactive steps, to activate, persist and create opportunities that bring about collective success through individual achievement specific to you. To write your story in this history, intentionally through the banner of love and unity.

I would like to start with a story of my own, the moment when I decided that I could be part of the change I wanted to see. I was privileged to sit at a conference in 2018 and listen to a speech delivered by President Paul Kagame, President of the Republic of Rwanda, where he made a very profound statement.

Until that moment I never really understood how it would stir me to action and revive in me a desire so deep that keeps alive my belief and determination to see the realisation of my dream for Africa. I hope by sharing my story at the beginning of this book with you it will do the same for you.

President Kagame made this simple yet powerful quote, then allowed it to linger on the screen, as he continued to move us through a journey of understanding the power of personal accountability for our realities.

"As Africans we need to do more, and doing more today is to significantly contribute to the funding and logistical requirements ... True, our means are limited, but surely not our ***willingness*** *and* ***commitment*** *to our continent and to the survival* ***of every single Member State of our Union****."*

– Paul Kagame

I have always been passionate about the continent and have seen opportunities for all, as many of us have. However, for me, that moment in time was one of those moments that lit a spark or better still, set ablaze a fire in me to act more intentionally **now** more than ever.

This is because until that moment I did not see myself as a significant enough part of the movement. Up to that point, I saw myself as a casual contributor and sometimes even an observer of the changes taking place in the continent, as if watching a news story, waiting and hoping to see the changes in the continent achieved by those with more means to do the work. This moment gave me the opportunity to change my perspective and be willing to commit to seeing the change. After I realised that it was my desire to see change in the continent, and that my love for my continent could drive it, I was and still am willing!

A determination was reborn in me and my desire and willingness to understand how I could make a difference to the continent and contribution to the funding and logistical requirements to support Agenda 2063 have continued to grow.

I felt the need to write this book to you now because 2023 makes 40 years until the fruition of Agenda 2063. This is within the lifetime of our generation! Forty years to freedom from the physical and mental slavery and colonisation that has for too long shackled the African people and nation. I truly hope this excites you as much as it does me!

In reading this book, I challenge you to read and use it personally. Understand that the beauty in books and revelation is really in how you make it yours. I have always been interested in perspectives and how they make the beauty in the world we see today.

If enough of us are willing to use our voices as one and bring together our differences and uniqueness, our passion, needs and requirements, we can make conscious changes together.

"Unity is strength, division is weakness."
- African Proverb

You can make a difference; Think of yourself as a heat seeking missile clearly identifying your specific uniqueness and contributions through each chapter of this book. There are many ways in which this may happen, but I believe that when read with the desire and determination to understand your mission in this vision, it will be shown to you.

I would like to emphasise that this book is in no way a replacement for the myriad of resources that the African Union and its member states have available which I would highly recommend. Rather, it seeks to serve as a directory to complementary material that will help guide you confidently to the initiatives, organisations, and materials for you.

As we start this journey, I am reminded of the saying that goes "When you are not familiar with fault lines, know enough to seek expert counsel before giving up". I am privileged to share throughout this book stories of those who have just like me been inspired by the vision of the future for Africa.

"However far a stream flows, it doesn't forget its origin."

It is my hope that these stories will add to the enthusiasm in knowing that this is for you, and it is not by a mere accident that you are reading this book today. May this knowledge empower us to continual growth as we see the joy in trial and failure, and make us strong enough to take up the mantle from the past and bravely walk towards the future.

When we see ourselves as a part of this chosen generation (Generation in the social context is generally defined as a group of people who were born and lived or are living around the same time), we allow ourselves to become just that, and in taking action the transformation begins.

"Tomorrow belongs to people who prepare for it today."
African Proverb

As we decide what action needs to be taken to show ourselves approved and grow in the trust that it will change, we will begin to see those changes one heart, one person, one village, and one member state at a time.

In this journey towards the realisation of Agenda 2063, we can draw on insightful wisdom distilled from *"The Art of Action by Stephen Bungay"* and guided by the principle of legacy thinking, we find ourselves at a pivotal juncture of deliberate action and strategic decisions. The ***40-year timeframe*** is getting ever closer, and so I implore you to embrace this call take action now in faith and enjoy the journey.

Within this arena of peaceful yet purposeful action, we are able to fully seize the helm of progress, eager to manifest our dedication and evolve in the steadfast belief that transformation is not only conceivable but **inevitable**. We are witnessing and continue to bear witness to this metamorphosis, not as an abstract notion, but as tangible shifts touching one heart, one individual, one community, and one member state at a time.

The legacy we are crafting through love is deeply rooted in purposeful actions, driven by unwavering determination, and fortified by the resilience to glean valuable insights from failure. Remember that innovation and progress arise from a series of what may first look like failures when in fact they were just steps in the journey.

As we close out this first chapter, consider the idea that "An inventor is almost always failing", but if failure was a stop sign, we would never see many of the inventions we see today. The key is determination to persevere and learning how to fail intelligently. Ground yourself in the knowledge that you can make a difference and be the change you want to see.

This process is about the unyielding determination to persevere and the art of failing with discernment. Determine for yourself in the conviction that you possess the agency to effect meaningful change and personify the transformation you aspire to witness.

Through this unwavering commitment to purposeful action and the indomitable spirit of resilience and excellence we shall shape the future we envisage for Africa and the global community.

Chapter 2

What Is Agenda 2063?

WHAT IS AGENDA 2063

Agenda 2063 is the African Union's blueprint and strategic framework for the ***transformation of Africa over a 50-year period***. That is in less than a lifetime, which makes this more exciting. In terms of the timeline, it is from 2013 to 2063, although it was officially adopted by the African Union (AU) in January 2015.

Agenda 2063 outlines a shared vision for the continent and its people and provides a roadmap for achieving the long-awaited vision of a prosperous and united Africa.

The African Union (AU) as an organisation was established on July 9, 2002 and serves as the continent's premier intergovernmental organisation, promoting unity, peace, and development in Africa. It succeeded the Organization of African Unity (OAU), which was founded on May 25, 1963.

The establishment of the AU is a tangible demonstration of multiple levels of integration, understanding and sharing through years of history and relationship building, cultural understanding and a deep desire to remain connected to building each and every member state in the union to truly see Africa as one.

"Landmark in African history and intentional shift in focus"

There was a bold transformation as the organisation pivoted from the OAU to the AU in what represented a landmark in

African history and an intentional shift in focus from political liberation and anti-colonialism to a broader agenda focusing on African unity of economic integration, development, and cooperation among African nations.

It is the beauty and complexity in the historic success and evolution of the African Union that gives me much hope to inspire you to be the change that we want to see in the continent by supporting the ambitions of the Agenda 2063.

It is worth noting that the origins of Agenda 2063 can be traced to many sources as the AU integrated historic documents and initiatives which led to their subsequent decision in 2013 to develop a guide for Africa's development. Through the development of Agenda 2063, the African Union has continued to seek the African Union Commission's (AUC) engagement with African citizens through multiple activities such as the "Year of Shared Values" in 2007.

This aims to include African citizens in shaping the future of the continent by bringing the ideas and initiatives of old and including the current ideas to build what we want to see in the future for the continent. Alongside this the AUC held consultations and discussions with various stakeholders, including civil society organisations, youth groups, women's organisations, academia, and the private sector to ensure that they increased the need for these different groups to know that they are essential to the building of the vision.

Africa's story has been written by others; we need to own our problems and solutions and write our story.
-Paul Kagame

The consultations culminated in the African Union Summit in January 2013, where the Assembly of Heads of State and Government of the African Union adopted Agenda 2063.

The vision and goals of Agenda 2063 were again further elaborated upon in order to tailor them to the intricacies of the member states through extensive consultations and engagement with these member states, regional economic communities, and other stakeholders.

This process saw the agenda becoming more understanding, free and focused, and united in goals and ambitions. It portrayed the way we want to see each other and the continent through finding the path to unity, oneness and development in the continent.

As the document draws inspiration from history through various documents and initiatives, including the African Union's Constitutive Act, the Lagos Plan of Action, the Abuja Treaty, the New Partnership for Africa's Development (NEPAD), the African Peer Review Mechanism, and the Millennium Development Goals (now replaced by the Sustainable Development Goals), we can understand that the goal was to truly bring understanding to the needs and requirements which would build an agenda that would start by causing internal transformation through its people and in that way sustainably build from within while drawing support from outside.

The vision of Agenda 2063 is

"To build an integrated, prosperous and peaceful Africa, driven by its own citizens and representing a dynamic force in the international arena."

"Write the vision and make it plain" is exactly the route that the African Union took with this mission – no small feat in bringing together this beautifully diverse continent. In amplifying some of the key words, we will be able to break it down in order to zoom into the vision of Agenda 2063.

build: *If you build something, you make it by joining things together. Synonyms: construct, make, raise.*

integrated*: Behave in such a way that they become part of the group or are accepted into it.*

Synonyms: *Unified, united, combined, leagued, combining, mixing, blending, harmony, inclusion, incorporation.*

prosperous: *people, places, and economies are rich and successful - wealthy, rich, affluent, well-off.*

peaceful: *In harmony, accord, agreement*

Africa **driven:** *determined and energetically led* by ***its own citizens*** and representing a ***dynamic force*** in the international arena.

Within this vision the focus is on seven (7) aspirations:

1. An integrated continent, politically united and based on the ideals of Pan-Africanism.

2. An Africa of good governance, respect for human rights, justice, and the rule of law.

3. A peaceful and secure Africa.

4. An Africa with a strong cultural identity, common heritage, values, and ethics.

5. A prosperous Africa based on inclusive growth and sustainable development.

6. An Africa whose development is people-driven, relying on the potential of its women and youth.

7. An Africa that is a strong, influential, and respected global player and partner.

In essence, the ambition of Agenda 2063 is to address the historical challenges faced by the continent through identifying and capitalising on its natural potential as a continent. Agenda

2063 is a comprehensive and ambitious plan for Africa's future. It recognises that the continent has faced significant challenges throughout history, but also acknowledges that there is great potential for growth and development. This potential lies not only in Africa's abundant natural resources, but also in its people.

The framework of Agenda 2063 aims to mobilise these resources by promoting regional integration, sustainable development, and active participation in the global arena. Every citizen, whether at a local or global level, has a role to play in achieving this vision. By continuously inspiring and empowering individuals, villages, and nations, we can ensure that the right people, opportunities, and places are available when they are needed most.

The African Union, through its member states and institutions, is responsible for implementing and monitoring the progress of Agenda 2063. This framework serves as a guide for national development plans and policies, encouraging coordination and collaboration among African countries to achieve a shared vision of a prosperous and united Africa by 2063. With commitment and dedication, we can make this vision a reality.

Chapter 3

Why Should I Care?

Are you rooted? *"The Decade of African Roots and Diaspora"*

WHY SHOULD I CARE?

The term Diaspora refers to a group of people who have been dispersed from their original homeland and have settled in various parts of the world. Historically, the term was used to describe the Jewish population which was forced to leave Israel and settle in other parts of the world after the Babylonian exile in the 6th century BCE.

Today, the term diaspora is used to describe any group of people who have migrated from their homeland and have established communities in other parts of the world. These communities often retain strong cultural ties to their original homeland and play an important role in promoting cultural diversity and cross-cultural understanding.

"In the history of the human race, those periods which later appeared as great have been the periods when the men and the women belonging to them had transcended the differences that divided them and had recognized in their membership in the human race a common bond."

- Haile Selassie I

The African Diaspora encompasses individuals and communities of African descent living outside the African continent – including those who have been historically dispersed due to the transatlantic slave trade, voluntary migrations, or other factors. It includes generations of people forcibly uprooted from their homeland and dispersed across the world.

The diaspora has formed vibrant communities, preserving cultural heritage and contributing to the development of various societies across the globe.

The Transatlantic Slave Trade and the African Diaspora

The transatlantic slave trade was a brutal system that forcibly transported millions of Africans to the Americas as slaves between the 16th and 19th centuries. Africans were captured, enslaved, and transported across the Atlantic Ocean, enduring inhumane conditions during the voyage known as the Middle Passage. This tragic chapter in history significantly impacted Africa.

The slave trade had many profound effects on Africa: the displacement and separation of families, the loss of cultural identity, and the erasure of ancestral connections. However, despite enduring immense suffering, enslaved Africans resiliently preserved elements of their heritage, such as music, dance, and religious practices, which continue to shape diasporic cultures today.

"If you are neutral in situations of injustice,
you have chosen the side of the oppressor."
-Desmond Tutu

One of the most enduring legacies of the African diaspora is the influence it has had on music. From the rhythms of West African drumming to the spirituals and blues of the American South, music has been a powerful means of expressing the joys and sorrows of the African experience. The sounds of the diaspora have been heard around the world, influencing genres as diverse as jazz, reggae, hip-hop, and Afrobeat.

Dance is another art form that has been shaped by the African diaspora. From the traditional dances of the people to the modern styles of breakdancing and krumping, dance has been a way for Africans to connect with their heritage and express themselves creatively.

Even in the face of oppression and violence, enslaved Africans found ways to dance and celebrate, often using dance as a form of resistance.

Despite the challenges of displacement and cultural erasure, the African Diaspora has managed to preserve and adapt its rich heritage. From the rhythms of the drum to the movements of the dance, the legacy of Africa can be seen and heard in the vibrant cultures of the diaspora.

The African Diaspora in Europe

Besides the transatlantic slave trade, Africans have also migrated to Europe throughout history and this being a part of my story. The reasons for this immigration are multifaceted and include colonial ties, economic opportunities, sanctions and political instability. Africans sought refuge, education, and employment in European countries, contributing to the cultural diversity and enrichment of these societies.

Many African countries have experienced political instability and conflict over the years, leading to large-scale emigration. Africans migrated to Europe in search of a better life, including fleeing war zones and persecution or the inability to remain in their home country due to sanctions reducing the availability of opportunities and access to food.

In addition, colonialism played a significant role in the migration of Africans to Europe by virtue of many African countries being colonised by European powers. The result of this was that Africans became integrated into European societies; they became aware of each other's differences and similarities in culture, tradition and food. This was insightful for me as I naturally found myself gravitating toward the food, music and culture that reminded me of my home and opened my eyes to a wider and more beautiful perspective of Africa through understanding the people.

This integration has led to the establishment of African diasporic communities in Europe, which have enriched the cultural landscape of these countries.

African artists, musicians, and writers have made significant contributions to the cultural scene in Europe, and African cuisine has become increasingly popular in many European cities. Despite facing challenges such as racism and discrimination, Africans in Europe have continued to thrive and make important contributions to their host countries.

The African Diaspora in Asia

The African Diaspora in Asia can be traced back to the ancient times when African traders and explorers first arrived in Asia. Over the years, the African community in Asia has grown significantly, with many Africans settling in countries like India, China, and Malaysia.

The experience of the African Diaspora in Asia has not always been positive. Many have faced discrimination and prejudice due to their skin colour and cultural differences. Despite these challenges, the African Diaspora in Asia has remained resilient and has made significant contributions to the cultural, social, and economic fabric of their respective countries.

Today, the African Diaspora in Asia continues to thrive, with a growing number of Africans migrating to the region for business, education, and other opportunities. As the world becomes more interconnected, the African Diaspora in Asia is poised to play an increasingly important role in shaping the future of both Africa and Asia.

The African Diaspora in Oceania

Throughout history, there has been a significant African Diaspora presence in Oceania. The migration of Africans to Oceania started as early as the 1700s when slaves were transported to countries such as Australia and New Zealand to work on plantations and farms. The descendants of these slaves then formed communities and contributed to the development of these countries.

In recent years, there has been an increase in the number of Africans migrating to Oceania for various reasons such as education, work opportunities, and family reunification. These individuals have brought with them their unique cultures, traditions, and languages, enriching the cultural diversity of Oceania.

Despite the contributions of Africans to Oceania, they still face challenges such as discrimination and prejudice. However, efforts are being made to address these issues and promote inclusivity and diversity in the region.

The Big Picture

As we can see, the picture of the global African Diaspora is just as intricate and vast as its home continent. Despite facing challenges such as discrimination and prejudice, the African Diaspora remains resilient, preserving their unique cultures and traditions, and contributing to the development of their host countries.

Countries like the USA, UK and Germany still celebrate and acknowledge the contribution of the Diaspora with Black History Month (BHM) being an example of an annual celebration and Black History being talked about and taught more openly.

"In the course of history, there comes a time when humanity is called to shift to a new level of consciousness, to reach a higher moral ground."
-Wangari Maathai (Environmentalist)

What does all this mean to us now?

Recognizing the potential of the diaspora as a valuable resource for Africa's development, Agenda 2063 acknowledges the importance of engaging and mobilising the diaspora to reach back past the separation and move forward into the place of unity through connecting to their roots and contributing to Africa's growth and development in a way in which calls you, because like I found out in 2018, it is the willingness and determination and alignment with your mission in this vision that changes the opportunities we see.

AU Aspiration 5: *An Africa with a strong cultural identity, common heritage, shared values and ethics*

The 6th region, although specific to the continent, has a global footprint. It is not a physical region like the other five regions of Africa (North, West, Central, East, and Southern Africa), it represents a recognition and inclusion of the African Diaspora as an important stakeholder in Africa's development and progress.

It offers the opportunity to see development and investment in the continent through different eyes. Through the eyes of understanding, the separation and lack of opportunities can be overcome so that we can rewrite the story not just now, but for the future generations.

The African Union (AU), an inspiration of vision and change, understands this and adopted the idea of the 6th Region in its Constitutive Act in 2000. The 6th Region concept emphasises the need for collaboration, solidarity, and cooperation between the African continent and its diaspora.

Embedded in the strategic framework of Agenda 2063 and recognised by the African Union is the "6th Region of Africa" This includes all people of African descent living outside of the African continent. This idea of a "6th Region" was specifically developed as a symbolic representation of the global African community and aims to share with the diaspora the call and our significance in shaping African history, culture, and future development and ensuring to include them in the continental objectives and aspirations to truly unify the continent.

Initiatives of the AU with the Diaspora

The AU has been working towards strengthening ties with the African Diaspora and fostering collaboration in various sectors.

The African continent is home to a wealth of resources and untapped potential. However, in order to fully unlock this potential, it is important to ensure that local communities are secure and able to maintain their identity whilst still having access to the skills, knowledge, and expertise necessary to drive sustainable development. This is where the diaspora can play a simple yet critical role through increasing demand; an example is embracing the beauty of African wear and materials or African chocolate, coffee or teas.

I sometimes question the reason why the beautiful designs and patterns of African wear have yet to fully embraced. There is so much beauty and quality in the materials in clothing, flavour in the coffees and teas and joy in purchasing these as many of them are locally produced, ethically sourced and quite unlike anything I have tasted anywhere else.

With the extensive reach of the diaspora as we discussed, the ability to increase demand for locally sourced products that resonates with both ethics and high quality standards is a movement we can all make today.

The technological age has given route to an easy method of purchasing, sourcing, mentorship, exchange programs, and partnerships with African institutions. The diaspora can help to transfer valuable skills and knowledge back to their home countries. This not only supports local development efforts, but also helps to build stronger ties between African communities both at home and abroad.

Another important aspect of this is the opportunity to give to the continent something many still do not have in the various sectors. A role model who continental and the diaspora can look up to and aspire to be like. By promoting the transfer of skills and knowledge, we can empower local communities to take control of their own development trajectories, and create a brighter future for all Africans.

Whether through entrepreneurship, education, or innovation, there are countless opportunities for the diaspora to make a meaningful impact in their home countries in the lives of people in the continent that holds the most youthful population in the world.

Cultural and intellectual exchange is crucial in promoting a deeper understanding and appreciation of different cultures, and in fostering mutual respect and tolerance. In the case of Africa, cultural exchange can help to showcase the diverse and rich heritage of the continent, and to combat negative stereotypes and misconceptions.

One way to facilitate cultural exchange is through the promotion of African cultural events, such as music festivals, art exhibitions, and dance performances. These events can provide a platform for African artists and cultural ambassadors to showcase their talents and share their experiences with a wider audience. Such events can also foster cross-cultural dialogue and understanding, as people from different backgrounds come together to enjoy and appreciate the richness and diversity of African culture.

Intellectual exchange is also important, as it can help to promote collaboration and innovation in various fields of study. The diaspora can play a key role in this, by sharing their knowledge and expertise with African institutions and researchers. This can lead to the development of new ideas and solutions to some of the pressing challenges facing the continent, such as poverty, inequality, and climate change.

According to the World Bank, remittances to low and middle-income countries reached a record high of $540 billion in 2020, despite the COVID-19 pandemic. This highlights the importance of diaspora remittances in supporting the livelihoods of families and communities in their home countries.

Governments and organisations have been exploring ways to harness these funds for productive investments and development projects. For example, some countries have established diaspora bonds, which are issued specifically to their citizens living abroad, to finance infrastructure and other development projects.

What this means in essence is that members of the diaspora can choose to invest intentionally into specific projects to ensure that we are building consciously for development and not just for consumerism.

There are organisations that have developed innovative financial products that allow diaspora members to invest in their home countries, such as mobile money transfer platforms that facilitate investment in small businesses or access to credit. Coming together as one to understand how to best utilise this opportunity is key in this sector.

The African Diaspora has always played a vital role in the continent's development. However, their contributions have often been sporadic and misaligned with the vision. To address this issue, policy engagement is crucial. Encouraging active participation of the diaspora in policy dialogues and decision-making processes can lead to more inclusive policies that take into account the perspectives and experiences of those living outside the continent. This can ultimately lead to better development outcomes for Africa.

By providing opportunities for the diaspora to contribute to policy formulation, governments and other stakeholders can tap into a wealth of knowledge and expertise.

Diaspora communities often have unique insights into the challenges facing their home countries, and can offer innovative solutions based on their experiences living abroad. Furthermore, involving the diaspora in policy dialogues can help to bridge the gap between the African continent and its global diaspora, promoting greater understanding and collaboration.

Overall, policy engagement is essential for harnessing the potential of the African diaspora. When the diaspora begins to actively engage and contribute to the policy-making process, we can help create more inclusive, effective policies that benefit all Africans, both on the continent and abroad.

I believe that the diaspora's contribution can be transformational and united and accelerate Agenda 2063 to full continental impact as the diaspora, strategically aligning their investments and business ventures with the goals of Agenda 2063 and work towards a common vision of a prosperous, peaceful, and integrated Africa.

Chapter 4

The Africa We Want

"An integrated, prosperous and peaceful Africa, driven by its own citizens, representing a dynamic force in the international arena"

"An integrated, prosperous and peaceful Africa, driven by its own citizens, representing a dynamic force in the international arena"

Addis Ababa, 26 January 2014: During the Ministerial retreat of the African Union's Executive Council being held in Bahir Dar, Ethiopia, from 24th to 26 January 2014, the Chairperson of the AU Commission, Dr Nkosazana Dlamini Zuma outlined her vision of Africa in 50 years' time, through "an email from the future". Written to a Kwame, a fictional character, in the year 2063, the full email is attached below.

This email provides some liberating insights and visions that I hope you catch on to as you read it as a vision of what is to come.

02

Agenda 2063

The AFRICA We Want

AUC Chairperson's E-mail from the Future

Addis Ababa, 26 January 2014:
During the Ministerial retreat of the African Union's Executive Council being held in Bahir Dar, Ethiopia, from 24th to 26 January 2014, the Chairperson of the AU Commission, Dr Nkosazana Dlamini Zuma outlined her vision of Africa in 50 years' time, through "an email from the future".

Written to a hypothetical Kwame in the year 2063, the full email is attached below:

Date	:	24 January 2063
To	:	Kwame@iamafrican.com
From	:	Nkosazana@cas.gov
Subject	:	African Unity

My dear friend Kwame,

Greetings to the family and friends, and good health and best wishes for 2063.

I write to you from the beautiful Ethiopian city of Bahir Dar, located on Lake Tana, as we finalize preparations for the Centenary celebrations of the Organisation of African Unity, which became the African Union in 2002 and laid the foundations for what is now our Confederation of African States (CAS).

Yes, who would have thought that the dream of Kwame Nkrumah and his generations, when they called in 1963 on Africans to unite or perish, would one day become a reality. And what a grand reality.

At the beginning of the twenty first century, we used to get irritated with foreigners when they treated Africa as one country: as if we were not a continent of over a billion people and 55 sovereign states! But, the advancing global trend towards regional blocks, reminded us that integration and unity is the only way for Africa to leverage its competitive advantage.

In fact, if Africa was one country in 2006, we would have been the 10th largest economy in the world! However, instead of acting as one, with virtually every resource in the world (land, oceans, minerals, energy) and over a billion people, we acted as fifty-five small and fragmented individual countries. The bigger countries that should have been the locomotives of African integration, failed to play their role at that time, and that is part of the reasons it took us so long. We did not realize our power, but instead relied on donors, that we euphemistically called partners.

That was the case in 2013, but reality finally dawned and we had long debates about the form that our unity should take: confederation, a united states, a federation or a union.

As you can see, my friend, those debates are over and the Confederation of African States is now twelve years old, launched in 2051.

What was interesting was the role played by successive generations of African youth. Already in 2013 during the Golden Jubilee celebrations, it was the youth that loudly questioned the slow progress towards integration. They formed

African Union Clubs in schools and universities across the continent, and linked with each other on social media. We thus saw the grand push for integration, for the free movement of people, for harmonization of education and professional qualifications, with the Pan African University and indeed the university sector and intelligentsia playing an instrumental role.

We were a youthful continent at the start of the 21st century, but as our youth bulge grew, young men and women became even more active, creative, impatient and assertive, often telling us oldies that they are the future, and that they (together with women) form the largest part of the electorates in all our countries!

Of course this was but one of the drivers towards unity. The accelerated implementation of the Abuja Treaty and the creation of the African Economic Community by 2034 saw economic integration moved to unexpected levels.

Economic integration, coupled with infrastructure development, saw intra-Africa trade mushrooming, from less than 12% in 2013 to approaching 50% by 2045. This integration was further consolidated with the growth of commodity exchanges and continental commercial giants. Starting with the African pharmaceutical company, Pan African companies now not only dominate our domestic market of over two billion people, but they have overtaken multi-nationals from the rest of the world in their own markets.

Even more significant than this, was the growth of regional manufacturing hubs, around the beneficiation of our minerals and natural resources, such as in the Eastern Congo, north-eastern Angola and Zambia's copper belt and at major Silicon valleys in Kigali, Alexandria, Brazzaville, Maseru, Lagos and Mombasa, to mention but a few such hubs.

My friend, Africa has indeed transformed herself from an exporter of raw materials with a declining manufacturing sector in 2013, to become a major food exporter, a global manufacturing hub, a knowledge centre, beneficiating our natural resources and agricultural products as drivers to industrialization.

Pan African companies, from mining to finance, food and beverages, hospitality and tourism, pharmaceuticals, fashion, fisheries and ICT are driving integration, and are amongst the global leaders in their sectors.

We are now the third largest economy in the world. As the Foreign Minister's retreat in Bahir Dar in January 2014 emphasised, we did this by finding the balance between market forces and strong and accountable developmental states and RECS to drive infrastructure, the provision of social services, industrialization and economic integration.

Let me recall what our mutual friend recently wrote:

"The (African) agrarian revolution had small beginnings. Successful business persons (and local governments) with roots in the rural areas started massive irrigation schemes to harness the waters of the continent's huge river systems. The pan-African river projects - on the Congo, the Nile, Niger, Gambia, Zambezi, Kunene, Limpopo and many others – financed by PPPs that involved African and BRIC investors, as well as the African Diaspora, released the continent's untapped agricultural potential.

By the intelligent application of centuries-old indigenous knowledge, acquired and conserved by African women who have tended crops in all seasons, within the first few years bumper harvests were being reported. Agronomists consulted women about the qualities of various grains – which ones survived low rainfalls and which thrived in wet weather; what pests threatened crops and how could they be combated without undermining delicate ecological systems.

The social impact of the agrarian revolution was perhaps the most enduring change it brought about. The status of women, the tillers of the soil by tradition, rose exponentially. The girl child, condemned to a future in the kitchen or the fields in our not too distant past, now has an equal chance of acquiring a modern education (and owning a farm or an agribusiness). African mothers today have access to tractors and irrigation systems that can be easily assembled.

The producers' cooperatives, (agribusinesses) and marketing boards these women established help move their produce and became the giant food companies we see today.'

We refused to bear the brunt of climate change and aggressively moved to promote the Green economy and to claim the Blue economy as ours. We lit up Africa, the formerly dark continent, using hydro, solar, wind, geo-thermal energy, in addition to fossil fuels.

And, whilst I'm on the Blue economy, the decision to form Africa-wide shipping companies, and encourage mining houses to ship their goods in vessels flying under African flags, meant a major growth spurt. Of course the decision taken in Dakar to form an African Naval Command to provide for the collective security of our long coastlines, certainly also helped.

Let me quote from our mutual friend again:

'Africa's river system, lakes and coast lines abound with tons of fish. With funding from the different states and the Diaspora, young entrepreneurs discovered... that the mouths of virtually all the rivers along the east coast are rich in a species of eel considered a delicacy across the continent and the world.

Clever marketing also created a growing market for Nile perch, a species whose uncontrolled proliferation had at one time threatened the survival of others in Lake Victoria and the Nile.

Today Namibia and Angola exploit the Benguela current, teaming with marine life, through the joint ventures funded by sovereign funds and the African Development Bank."

On the east coast, former island states of Seychelles, Comoros, Madagascar and Mauritius are leading lights of the Blue economy and their universities and research institutes attract marine scientists and students from all over the world.

Dear friend, you reminded me in your last e-mail how some magazine once called us 'The hopeless continent', citing conflicts, hunger and malnutrition, disease and poverty as if it was a permanent African condition. Few believed that our pledge in the 50th Anniversary Declaration to silence the guns by 2020 was possible. Because of our firsthand experience of the devastation of conflicts, we tackled the root causes, including diversity, inclusion and the management of our resources.

If I have to single out one issue that made peace happened, it was our commitment to invest in our people, especially the empowerment of young people and women. By 2013 we said Africa needed a skills revolution and that we must change our education systems to produce young people that are innovative and entrepreneurial and with strong Pan African values.

From early childhood education, to primary, secondary, technical, vocational and higher education – we experienced a true renaissance, through the investments we made, as governments and the private sector in education and in technology, science, research and innovation.

Coupled with our concerted campaigns to eradicate the major diseases, to provide access to health services, good nutrition, energy and shelter, our people indeed became and are our most important resource. Can you believe it my friend, even the dreaded malaria is a thing of the past.

Of course this shift could not happen without Africa taking charge of its transformation, including the financing of our development. As one esteemed Foreign minister said in 2014: Africa is rich, but Africans are poor.

With concerted political determination and solidarity, and sometimes one step back and two steps forward, we made financing our development and taking charge of our resources a priority, starting with financing the African Union, our democratic elections and our peacekeeping missions.

The Golden Jubilee celebrations were the start of a major paradigm shift, about taking charge of our narrative.

Agenda 2063, its implementation and the milestones it set, was part of what brought about this shift. We developed Agenda 2063 to galvanize and unite in action all Africans and the Diaspora around the common vision of a peaceful, integrated and prosperous Africa. As an overarching framework, Agenda 2063 provided internal coherence to our various sectoral frameworks and plans adopted under the OAU and AU. It linked and coordinated our many national and regional frameworks into a common continental transformation drive.

Planning fifty years ahead, allowed us to dream, think creatively, and sometimes crazy as one of the Ministers who hosted the 2014 Ministerial retreat said, to see us leapfrog beyond the immediate challenges.

Anchored in Pan Africanism and the African renaissance, Agenda 2063 promoted the values of solidarity, self-belief, non-sexism, self-reliance and celebration of our diversity.

As our societies developed, as our working and middle classes grew, as women took their rightful place in our societies, our recreational, heritage and leisure industries grew: arts and culture, literature, media, languages, music and film. WEB du Bois grand project of Encyclopedia Africana finally saw the light and Kinshasha is now the fashion capital of the world.

From the onset, the Diaspora in the traditions of Pan Africanism, played its part, through investments, returning to the continent with their skills and contributing not only to their place of origin, but where the opportunities and needs were found.

Let me conclude this e-mail, with some family news. The twins, after completing their space studies at Bahir Dar university, decided to take the month before they start work at the African Space Agency to travel the continent. My old friend, in our days, trying to do that in one month would have been impossible!

But, the African Express Rail now connects all the capitals of our former states, and indeed they will be able to crisscross and see the beauty, culture and diversity of this cradle of humankind. The marvel of the African Express Rail is that it is not only a high speed-train, with adjacent highways, but also contains pipelines for gas, oil and water, as well as ICT broadband cables: African ownership, integrated planning and execution at its best!

The continental rail and road network that now crisscross Africa, along with our vibrant airlines, our spectacular landscapes and seductive sunsets, the cultural vibes of our cities, make tourism one of our largest economic sectors.

Our eldest daughter, the linguist, still lectures in KiSwahili in Cabo Verde, at the headquarters of the Pan African Virtual University. KiSwahili is now a major African working language, and a global language taught at most faculties across the world. Our grand children still find it very funny how we used to struggle at AU meetings with English, French and Portuguese interpretations, how we used to fight the English version not in line with the French or Arabic. Now we have a lingua franca, and multi-lingualism is the order of the day.

Remember how we used to complain about our voice not being heard in trade negotiations and the Security Council, how disorganized, sometimes divided and nationalistic we used to be in those forums, how we used to be summoned by various countries to their capitals to discuss their policies on Africa?

How things have changed. The Confederation last year celebrated twenty years since we took our seat as a permanent member of the UN Security Council, and we are a major force for global stability, peace, human rights, progress, tolerance and justice.

My dear friend, I hope to see you next month in Haiti, for the second round of unity talks between the Confederation of African States and the Caribbean states. This is a logical step, since Pan Africanism had its roots amongst those early generations, as a movement of Africans from the mother continent and the Diaspora for liberation, self-determination and our common progress.

I end this e-mail, and look forward to seeing you in February. I will bring along some of the chocolates from Accra that you so love, which our children can now afford.

Till we meet again, Nkosazana.

Do you see the vision of Africa we see?

This email from the future, penned by an imagined AUC Chairperson in 2063, vividly portrays Africa's remarkable transformation over the years. It starts by reflecting on the historical establishment of the African Union (AU) and its evolution into the Confederation of African States (CAS) in 2051. The narrative emphasises how unity and integration have become essential for Africa to harness its full potential on the global stage.

The email highlights the crucial role played by ***successive generations of African youth in advocating*** for integration and unity. It underscores the progression from fragmented nations to a united, economically integrated, and globally influential African entity. Economic integration, infrastructure development, and growth in intra-African trade significantly *contributed* to this shift, establishing Africa as a major player in various sectors.

However, the truth is that we cannot empower what we do not know; it is time for us to intentionally educate ourselves and use this knowledge and vision as a driver for the changes that we are going to see.

I greatly appreciate how intricate, detailed and visionary the email is. It mentions the remarkable advances in agriculture, energy, and fisheries, driven by indigenous knowledge and sustainable practices. In the email, Africa embraced renewable energy sources and prioritised the blue economy, harnessing the potential of its abundant rivers, lakes, and coastlines. With technology today, the continent is making strides in education, healthcare, and skills development, prioritising its people as the most valuable resource seems doable in much less than the 40 years given to us to walk through, if we want to.

We can see how this vision emphasises Africa's active involvement in shaping its narrative and taking charge of its own transformation, through breaking free from negative stereotypes, both mental and physical. The role of the African Diaspora, with its investments and contributions, is underscored, depicting a collaborative approach to African progress. The narrative ends by alluding to the vibrant linguistic and cultural diversity that characterises Africa, showcasing the continent's newfound unity and collective strength on the global stage.

As we walk into the reality of some of these movements in the present day, the summary for me is that Yes, African Union's Agenda 2063 does matter to the everyday person and we matter to it.

Agenda 2063 is a comprehensive development framework that primarily focuses on the long-term transformation of the African continent, its aspirations, goals, and actions have direct implications for the lives of individuals in their *daily realities*.

Taking consistent and purposeful action is crucial for the actions in this agenda taking form, it is a living document that upon personal and united transformation becomes our reality. Ideas and plans alone are not enough; they must be accompanied by action.

"If you think you're too small to make a difference, try spending the night with a mosquito."
– African Proverb

The power of vision and people's ability to imagine and create cannot be taken for granted.

When visionary projects such as this one are ready to be realised. There is a collective influence, strength, and potential that individuals possess when they come together for a common purpose. When people unite, collaborate, and work towards a shared goal, the ripple effects that they can create are significant and affect positive change in various aspects of life, including social, political, economic, and environmental.

Movements and revolutions throughout history have demonstrated the power of people when it comes to challenging existing systems, fighting for justice, advocating for human rights, and bringing about social and political transformations. This is already evident in the continent through the transformation of the colonial history of the continent to independent countries.

People drive social change by raising awareness, mobilising communities, and influencing public opinion. This can and is done effectively through grassroots initiatives and activism, individuals raise and address issues such as inequality, discrimination, poverty, and environmental degradation. By promoting a more equitable and sustainable society, different views are met, as things which are visible to you may not be visible to everyone but once executed upon it can be clearly seen by all –this is the beauty of vision.

When people who have a shared goal come together, they can spark innovation and drive progress. This is the power of uniting under the strategic framework of Agenda 2063 which tactically sees the opportunity in every spectrum of society. Collaborative efforts in fields such as science, technology, history, arts, and entrepreneurship have led to ground-breaking discoveries, advancements, and creations that have improved the quality of life for many.

It is important to understand that we are the masters of our fate because we have the power to control our thoughts and determine our actions. It is up to each of us as individuals to decide how much things matter and how much energy we wish to put into them. This is an area that requires strategic alignment for every individual, country and business.

Cultural and social Identity is something that is so detailed in terms of the diversity within the African context. I like the quote from the "Insights into the center of gravity of a business and hence innovative strategies come from people of long experience who have an unusual capacity to reflect on that experience in such a way that they become aware of the patterns it shows". Agenda 2063 acknowledges the importance of preserving and promoting Africa's cultural heritage and social identity for all 6 regions.

In the email from the future, "chocolates from Ghana" are mentioned. This excites me, as we now position Africa not only to be independent but to be a global powerhouse. Some of the largest global cocoa-producing countries include Ivory Coast (Côte d'Ivoire) and Ghana. These countries are significant sources of cocoa beans for the global chocolate industry. If chocolates made from cocoa beans grown in these regions were locally produced and globally distributed, the vision of a global African chocolate brand seems inevitable and more so an emergence of innovations and grand recipes showcasing traditional delights.

We can understand how deeply Agenda 2063 recognizes the value of cultural diversity, arts, and heritage in fostering social cohesion, pride, and unity among African societies. I emphasise so much on chocolates because the beauty and taste of fresh locally produced goods is yet to be understood and truly appreciated.

Understanding and empowering the recognition of social and cultural identity across the continent will not only make us stronger but bring us back to a core of true oneness and unity. The beauty, ability and flexibility in Agenda 2063 to maintain the uniqueness and individuality of our nations, tribes and cities but also to unite us both as local people in the continent, and as a global diaspora to contribute to a sense of belonging and cultural preservation as individuals will surely bring with it true unity.

How this works is key to the integration of the continent. It is true that this is no easy feat as it has been estimated that there are anywhere from 2,000 to 3,000 distinct ethnic groups in Africa. These groups can be further divided into smaller tribes or sub-groups, each with its own unique language, customs, and traditions. Additionally, globalisation, urbanisation, and other social factors have led to cultural blending and the emergence of hybrid identities in many areas. Despite this, there is great potential for continued understanding and integration.

Adopting a positive mindset can transform your perspective and open doors to new possibilities.

Social identity is key, but can only be cultivated through the positive optimism, inclusion and self-belief in the value of every society. These societies need to know that they matter and are a part of the identity of the continent. By speaking up, we are essentially bringing into the picture a unique attribute that can cause an effect on a generation and bring in part of society that may not have otherwise been reached. What a beautiful vision – to reach the ones that may have felt forgotten with the same opportunities and access as if they were in a major city through the power of integration with technology.

Agenda 2063 aims to promote inclusive and sustainable development, which directly impacts the quality of life for individuals. The agenda's focus on poverty eradication, access to healthcare, education, clean water, infrastructural development, and social protection programs which contribute to improved living conditions and well-being.

Alongside this, the creation of employment is paramount in Agenda 2063, with it recognising the importance of creating employment opportunities and promoting economic growth.

Implementation of the agenda's initiatives, such as promoting entrepreneurship, developing strategic sectors, and enhancing regional integration, can foster economic opportunities and job creation, providing individuals with sustainable livelihoods.

Developing the receptivity of people to these opportunities is essential for growth and transformation in order to activate the potential that is within. For individuals, this involves understanding strengths, weaknesses, values, and beliefs and giving opportunities that align with your authentic self and shape your destiny and that of the continent accordingly but also yourself by locating your core strength.

"One of my passions is education and skills development in both this and the next generation."

Access to information is now easier than ever and this brings with it the opportunity to transform the access to good quality education through the power of the internet. Anyone across the globe and the continent can access the same level of information as the other. Enhancing access to quality education, vocational training, and lifelong learning opportunities can empower individuals to acquire relevant skills and knowledge, increasing their employability and enabling personal development.

This ability for us to be continuously learning and adding to this our experiences and emotion allows us to adapt to change, acquire new insights, and enhance our capabilities.

One of the most exciting things that I have had the privilege to see and be a part of is the focus on gender equality, the empowerment of women, and enhanced youth participation in various spheres including technology, education, employment, leadership, and decision-making. This focus on inclusivity and empowerment directly benefits not just women and young people in their everyday lives, but everyone as it brings to the global picture diversity of thought additional support for the execution of additional power resources.

This opportunity to include different perspectives allows us to nurture meaningful relationships and networks by surrounding ourselves with supportive and like-minded individuals who can provide guidance, inspiration, and open our creative ability to see opportunities. This helps execution and decision making as we become more aligned with all local business through strategic goals and ambitions of the Agenda 2063.

Building connections expands your sphere of influence and can open doors that lead to new pathways in shaping your destiny.

It's the little things citizens do. That's what will make the difference.
-Wangari Maathai

Infrastructure plays a big part in quality of life as it provides ease of access. Agenda 2063 and developments have started with all means of transport and infrastructural development across the continent which has many facets including transportation, energy, and information and communication technology. This improved infrastructure can enhance connectivity, facilitate trade, and provide access to essential services, benefiting countries, villages and individuals through increased availability of transportation, communication, and access to markets.

Although this can already feel like a huge understatement, I am reminded of thinkers, missionaries and investors that changed the world. To conclude this chapter, consider the idea that many times, when launching a long-term project just like the Agenda 2063, the planner often knows that it is typical not to have everything that is needed at the start.

When an engineer building a plane understands that they will need components along the way of things that just do not exist, this does not stop them from pursuing the vision, no. Instead, they continue to work in the present and this generates the pieces of the puzzle that are seen and then gives rise to inspiration and structure to build out those that are unseen.

Action without thought is empty. Thought without action is blind.
– Kwame Nkrumah

Be encouraged in knowing that what you have is valuable and you can start today. The desire to be a part of one of the goals mentioned in the previous chapter shall be seen. Hold on to it like a thread that takes you through this book and leads you to the activities and actions which can bring your desire to actualisation.

Clarifying your purpose and creating a compelling vision for your life can give you direction and guide your actions. When you have a clear sense of purpose, it becomes easier to make decisions and take steps that move you closer to your desired destiny.

Chapter 5

The Commitment of Africa

Although opportunities for Africa have always existed, there is a difference today. Work has been done, movement has been made and there is a continued and increasing commitment from African countries, regional institutions, and stakeholders to implement Agenda 2063.

Here are some key factors that contribute to the potential for Agenda 2063 to materialise:

Africa must revert to what it was before the imperialists divided it. These are artificial divisions which we, in our pan-African concept, will seek to remove.

President Robert Mugabe

Today politics in Africa is emerging as this unification brings with it stability and integration. There is strong political will among African leaders to drive the implementation of Agenda 2063. Many countries have aligned their national development plans with the agenda and have established institutional frameworks to oversee its implementation. This commitment increases the likelihood of progress towards the agenda's goals.

Furthermore, the African Union has taken steps to ensure that the implementation of Agenda 2063 remains a priority. The African Union Commission, in partnership with various stakeholders, has developed a monitoring and evaluation framework to track progress towards the achievement of the agenda's goals.

Through this framework, African countries can identify areas that require improvement and take appropriate measures to address them.

In addition to political will, the successful implementation of Agenda 2063 also requires the active participation of civil society, the private sector, and other stakeholders. The African Union recognizes the importance of these groups in driving sustainable development and has created spaces for their engagement in the implementation process. This approach ensures that the agenda reflects the needs and aspirations of all Africans and that progress towards its goals is inclusive and equitable.

One of the key benefits of regional integration and cooperation is the promotion of intra-African trade. By working together to develop infrastructure and harmonise policies, countries can increase the flow of goods and services between each other, boosting economic growth and development.

Additionally, collaboration can help to address common challenges that are faced by countries across the continent, such as climate change, conflict, and poverty. Through the African Union and other regional economic communities, African countries can leverage their collective strength to achieve common goals and improve the lives of their citizens.

Overall, regional integration and cooperation are essential for Africa's continued growth and prosperity.

Policy Engagement: Agenda 2063 aims to increase the involvement of the diaspora in policy dialogues and decision-making processes that affect Africa's development. It provides opportunities for the diaspora to contribute their perspectives, insights, and experiences to shape policies and strategies at the continental, regional, and national levels.

How long should you hang out in the mirror?
Until you see His face in it!

While Agenda 2063 provides a strategic framework at the continental level, the specific policies and initiatives for diaspora engagement can vary among different African countries. Each country has the flexibility to develop its own policies and programs based on their specific context and priorities. Here are a few examples of diaspora policies and initiatives implemented by some African countries within the context of Agenda 2063:

Our children may learn about the heroes of
the past. Our task is to make ourselves
architects of the future
– Jomo Kenyatta

Ethiopia: The Ethiopian government launched the Ethiopian Diaspora Agency (EDA) in 2013 to strengthen ties with the Ethiopian Diaspora and facilitate their engagement in the country's development. The EDA provides various services such as investment facilitation, capacity building, and support for diaspora philanthropy initiatives. Additionally, Ethiopia has implemented initiatives like the Diaspora Trust Fund to encourage diaspora contributions to development projects.

Ghana: The Government of Ghana established the Diaspora Affairs Bureau under the Ministry of Foreign Affairs and Regional Integration to engage with the Ghanaian diaspora. The bureau focuses on facilitating diaspora investments, promoting diaspora tourism, and providing support for diaspora engagement in sectors such as healthcare, education, and technology transfer.

Nigeria: The Nigerian government established the Nigerians in Diaspora Commission (NiDCOM) in 2017 to harness the potential of the Nigerian diaspora for national development. NiDCOM facilitates diaspora investments, skills transfer, and supports diaspora contributions to sectors like agriculture, healthcare, and education. The commission also organises the Nigerian Diaspora Investment Summit to promote investment opportunities for the diaspora.

Senegal: Senegal established the Directorate of Senegalese Abroad (DASE) to strengthen engagement with the Senegalese diaspora. DASE focuses on promoting diaspora investments, entrepreneurship, and skills transfer. It provides various services such as financial and technical support for diaspora projects, facilitation of land acquisition for investment purposes, and cultural exchange programs.

Rwanda: The Rwandan government has implemented several initiatives to engage with the Rwandan diaspora. This includes programs like the Rwanda Global Diaspora Convention, which brings together Rwandans from around the world to explore investment opportunities and contribute to national development.

The government also provides support for diaspora entrepreneurs, skills transfer programs, and facilitates diaspora participation in policy dialogues.

Chapter 6

Empowered To Take Space?

The spirit of empowerment and inclusion is inherent in the agenda's objectives and aspirations. Agenda 2063 seeks to empower all Africans, including those in the diaspora, to actively participate and contribute to Africa's development.

Your willingness to look at your darkness is
what empowers you to change.

- Iyanla Vanzant

Agenda 2063 emphasises that Africa's development should be people-driven. It recognizes the importance of empowering African citizens, including those in the diaspora, to actively participate in the decision-making processes and contribute their skills and expertise. There is opportunity to support and empower for mutual benefit for both individuals and global companies.

Women and youth have been supported for many years through the majority workplace presence of men across the continent and the world at large. It is time they were more supported in order to drive forward the goals. Agenda 2063 places a strong focus on empowering women and youth.

It seeks to create opportunities for women and youth to actively participate in all sectors of society, including politics, governance, and economic activities. This empowerment extends to the diaspora, as efforts are made to engage and mobilise the diaspora's talents by including women and youth in Africa's development.

AU Aspiration 6: *An Africa, whose development is people-driven, relying on the potential of African people, especially its women and youth, and caring for children.*

There are countless organisations across the continent looking to engage diaspora support in developing a global force to be more equitable, diverse and inclusive. Connecting the global picture to the diaspora, we can help develop faster through mentorship and role models. As we mutually educate and edify each other through our experiences, we empower each other to break through to another perspective and the ability to see opportunities.

Agenda 2063 aims to achieve inclusive growth and development that benefits all Africans. It emphasises the need to bridge gaps and address inequalities in various aspects, such as education, healthcare, and access to resources and opportunities. This inclusive approach extends to the diaspora, as efforts are made to ensure their participation and inclusion in Africa's development processes.

Equally important is promoting Africa's cultural identity and heritage. In the chapter “Why Should I Care”, we got to understand the diverse reach of the diaspora across the globe. We have seen how they have maintained and empowered their cultural identity. Agenda 2063 encourages the diaspora to actively contribute to the preservation and promotion of African culture and heritage, thus empowering them to embrace and share their cultural identities through a global identity of the African people.

The Third World is a state of the mind and until we change our attitude as Africans, if there is a fourth, fifth and even sixth world, we will be in it.
— Patrice L.O. Lumumba

Chapter 7

The Largest Free Trade Area in The World

The African Continental Free Trade Area (AfCFTA) is a major step towards enhancing regional integration and trade among African countries. It will create the world's largest free trade area, encompassing a market of over 1.2 billion people (not including the diaspora) with a combined GDP of more than $3 trillion. In the strength of this commitment, the AU has increased the momentum of this campaign by declaring 2023 the "Year of AfCFTA: Acceleration of the African Continental Free Trade Area Implementation"

This was shared at the AU Summit this year:

"The AfCFTA is a gamechanger for the African continent and year 2023 presents yet another opportunity to strengthen partnerships, mobilise resources, undertake outreach activities and promote the ***utilisation*** *of the AfCFTA by economic operators through unceasing engagement that will sustain the high momentum around the AfCFTA.*

Beyond the continent, the Theme of the Year 2023 is expected to strengthen the role of the African Diaspora, People of African Descent and create a meaningful life between the implementation of the AfCFTA and the Decade of African Roots and Diaspora (2021-2032) by driving initiatives aimed at bringing together, projects, events and other initiatives to strengthen the role of these group in advancing the economic integration of the AfCFTA."

By eliminating tariffs and other trade barriers, AfCFTA will make it easier and more cost-effective for businesses to operate across borders. This will encourage investment and job creation, while also promoting the development of regional value chains and increasing the competitiveness of African economies. However, the success of AFCTA will depend on the willingness of African countries to collaborate and implement the necessary reforms to facilitate cross-border trade.

Chapter 8

What Opportunities are There for The Diaspora?

In the middle of this book, I want to go back to where I started as a reminder that as a member of the diaspora that started the journey with the call to action and even conviction, I experienced through sitting through a speech with Paul Kagame.

"As Africans we need to do more, And doing more today is to significantly contribute to the funding and logistical requirements ... True, our means are limited, but surely not our willingness and commitment to our continent and to the survival of every single Member State of our Union."

These words from President Paul Kagame resonated with me deeply and still ring true today. As someone who has lived outside of Africa for some of my life, I have often felt a sense of longing to connect more deeply and produce fruit through my roots. The African Union has themed 2021 to 2032 *the Decade of African Roots and Diaspora (2021-2032).* Listening to President Kagame's call to action, I was reminded of the importance of the power of now and staying connected to our homeland and contributing to its growth and development.

AU Aspiration 7: Africa as a strong, united, resilient and influential global player and partner.

It may seem daunting to navigate the widespread opportunities in Africa, however, it is our willingness and commitment that will help us seek and find the truth and our call as individuals. The African Union offers all 6 regions various avenues to connect through this decade, which when supported, will help open up the right opportunities to you.

Personally, this year I have taken time to intentionally re-educate myself and have come to see the many benefits that connecting to your core and strategically aligning yourself with the mission can yield. We can all play a part in building a brighter future for our continent, its people and the world at large.

Whether through financial support, business ventures, volunteering, or simply spreading awareness, every action counts. I am proud to be part of the African Diaspora, and I am motivated to do my part in realising the vision for a stronger, more prosperous Africa.

I believe and I hope after all I have shared, that you now understand that Agenda 2063 acknowledges the African Diaspora as a valuable resource and acknowledges the potential for their engagement in Africa's development as a people in the knowledge and hope that as we support each other in the spirit of unity and excellence, the change we want to see will happen practically.

In exploring the concept of unity for Africa's advancement, we draw upon a powerful principle illustrated in ancient texts.

Do not be afraid, for those who are with us
are more than those who are with them.

-Elisha son of Shaphat, c.850 BCE

The idea that a small number can overcome great odds when unified echoes through historical accounts. As we reflect on this principle in the context of Africa's development, particularly Agenda 2063, its profound relevance becomes apparent.

I admire the freedom fighters, activists, thought leaders and prophets that have gone before us to light the way for all to see. The vision to reunite Africa, discarding past divisions, strongly echoes this timeless principle, emphasising the imperative of shared vision and unity.

Unity of a continent as the proposed strategy underscores the imperative of embracing and understanding Africa's diversity, akin to the timeless principle.

Finding the core and root of who you are should be an ambition of every African and human in this decade the Diaspora marches not only towards 2063 but 2032 "***the Decade of African Roots and Diaspora (2021-2032)***"

In finding these roots, may we be empowered through revelation and understanding and engage in the initiatives set out by the AU.

Here are some of the initiatives:

- Provide an international showcase for the programming of cultural events proposed by the various countries within the framework of the agenda of the decade

- Promote meetings between African artists and members of Afro-descendant and diasporic communities

- Support projects dedicated to the research, conservation, restoration and rehabilitation of African heritage.

- Encourage the development of international exchanges through cultural, artistic and tourism businesses, sources of employment for African youth.

By nurturing collective understanding and fostering a shared vision, Africa can draw strength from its diverse resources. Actively involving the diaspora and leveraging their *unique perspectives, skills, and exper*iences, we endeavour to harness a collective force propelling the continent towards a prosperous future. As we embrace these opportunities and *shed artificial divisions* and embrace the ancient principle, collective strength, guided by a unified vision, shall drive Africa forward, achieving the aspirations outlined in Agenda 2063.

Through these collaborations and partnerships, Agenda 2063 aims to leverage the skills, expertise, and resources of the African diaspora to drive the continent's development agenda forward. African governments, by working together, will find that there are several opportunities to create mutually beneficial relationships that promote sustainable development and economic growth across the continent.

One example of such collaboration is the African Diaspora Investment Symposium (ADIS), which brings together African governments, businesses, and the diaspora to explore investment opportunities and form partnerships.

Through events like ADIS, the diaspora can share their knowledge and experiences while also learning more about the economic and business landscape in Africa.

Identifying the best opportunities for growth is a complex and dynamic process that can vary depending on various factors such as economic conditions, industry trends, technological advancements, and regional contexts. Strategic Alignment is key for success of this application and even more so when building a visionary company.

One of the key ways in which the African continent can benefit from the diaspora is through economic cooperation. By encouraging diaspora investment and entrepreneurship in Africa, we can create more job opportunities, spur economic growth and development, and foster innovation and creativity. In order to achieve this, it is important to create a conducive environment that provides support mechanisms for diaspora-led initiatives.

This can include things like tax incentives, access to funding and financing, and streamlined regulatory processes. By working together in this way, we can tap into the immense potential of the diaspora and harness its power to drive positive change on the continent.

"Thoughts are things and powerful things when they are mixed with definiteness of purpose, persistence and a burning desire for their translation into riches or other objects!"

There is a balance between seizing opportunities on the spur of the moment, and understanding that by persisting under the vision will bring our desire to maturity, and eventually fruition.

Acting now allows you to seize the moment and take advantage of favourable circumstances that could lead to success, advancement, or personal fulfilment. This is seen in the African Union's inclusion of all the various parts of their unions to initialise the plan.

One of the truest tests of integrity is its blunt refusal to be compromised.
-Chinua Achebe

The African Diaspora brings a specialised knowledge to the continent through their experience of diverse cultural insights. The global concept here refers to diasporas from various countries uniting under one umbrella with the common theme of currently being located out of the continent – ***the region in the air.*** Through this virtual community, the diaspora and local citizens can unite to share specialised knowledge and skills and together channel their combined energy and resources into building the continent.

Chapter 9

Technology And the Digital Revolution

It would be remiss not to mention the opportunity that has arrived in time to excel Africa Forward. Africa stands at the forefront of a digital revolution, showcasing the immense potential of technology to revolutionise not just the continent but the entire world. The transformative power of digital technology encompasses a spectrum of innovations and advancements which are reshaping the way people are able to envision and embrace progress.

This is not merely about adopting technology; it's about utilising it for its highest good and regulating it whilst enabling a profound shift in mindset, culture, and processes, essential to unlock its full potential not just in Africa but in the global community.

As the world becomes more connected through technology, digital transformation is increasingly being viewed as a key driver of economic growth. This is particularly true in Africa, where the potential for digital innovation is enormous. From mobile banking to e-commerce, digital technology is transforming the way people live, work, and do business across the continent.

With a young, tech-savvy population and a growing middle class, Africa is poised to take advantage of this digital revolution in ways that were previously unimaginable.

However, there are also challenges that must be overcome. One of the biggest obstacles is the digital divide, which refers to the gap between those who have access to technology and those who do not. In Africa, this divide is particularly stark, with many people lacking even basic access to the internet. To address this issue, governments and organisations are working to increase connectivity and provide digital skills training to underserved communities.

Despite these challenges, there is no doubt that digital transformation has the potential to introduce significant positive change for Africa to benefit from this transformative technological revolution.

It is important to note that digital transformation is not just about implementing technology. It also involves a shift in mindset, culture, and processes to fully realise the potential of technology. This requires investment in training employees, creating a supportive environment for experimentation and innovation, and developing a clear digital strategy that aligns with their overall business objectives. It requires governments to put in place regulations and guidance on uses and ensure local and cultural inputs in these technologies. Technology touches almost every sector of society. As an indication of what I mean, let us look at a few examples.

The Environment and Digital Technology

As the demand for energy continues to rise, the need to shift towards sustainable and clean energy sources becomes more pressing. Renewable energy sectors such as solar, wind, hydro, and geothermal power are becoming increasingly important in meeting this demand.

Africa stands as a beacon of environmental friendliness on a global scale. The continent is progressively embracing renewable energy and clean technologies, paving the way for a sustainable future. Notably, solar, wind, hydro, and geothermal power are gaining prominence as viable energy sources, highlighting Africa's dedication to a green energy revolution.

Beyond simply meeting energy requirements, these clean technologies and energy efficiency solutions are pivotal in curbing greenhouse gas emissions and combating climate change.

Additionally, promoting green infrastructure, such as green roofs, permeable pavements, and urban forests, further amplifies efforts to alleviate the urban heat island effect, combat air pollution, and promote biodiversity.

The strategic investment in renewable energy and clean technologies has the potential to not only elevate Africa's environmental stewardship but also unlock substantial economic opportunities.

The renewable energy sector could foster job creation, stimulate innovation, and attract significant investment. Embracing a transition towards a cleaner and more sustainable energy system promises a brighter future, fostering improved health, greater prosperity, and enhanced equity for all.

Healthcare

The healthcare sector offers growth opportunities, especially in areas such as telemedicine, digital health solutions, pharmaceutical manufacturing, medical devices, and healthcare infrastructure development.

The COVID-19 pandemic has further highlighted the importance of the healthcare sector. The need for telemedicine and digital health solutions has become even more apparent as people have tried to limit physical contact.

The development of pharmaceutical and medical devices is also crucial in the fight against the virus. As a result, the healthcare sector has become an attractive investment opportunity. The growth potential of the sector is further supported by the increasing focus on healthcare infrastructure development in many countries. This is aimed at improving access to healthcare services for all, including those in rural areas.

Infrastructural Development

Africa has a rich history of infrastructure development, with ancient civilizations like Egypt and Zimbabwe building impressive structures that still stand today. By combining this historical wisdom with modern expertise through technology, Africa is creating a sustainable and efficient infrastructure network that will support economic growth and development for generations to come.

Technology in Agriculture

Furthermore, investing in agribusiness and food processing can also contribute to the development of rural communities and help reduce poverty. Products of technology such as drones are revolutionising the air space by providing farmers with access to modern technology and equipment, they can increase their yields, improve the quality of their produce, and earn more income.

Additionally, by establishing food processing facilities, countries can add value to their raw agricultural commodities and create new products for domestic and international markets, thereby increasing their export potential.

This can lead to economic growth and stability, as well as enhancing food security by ensuring a steady supply of nutritious food. Overall, investing in agribusiness and food processing can have far reaching benefits for the well-being of both the economy and the population.

This one is actually very close to my heart as we strive to not only unshackle minds but ensure that food poverty is non-existent across the continent. Growing up Zimbabwe, long been celebrated as the "breadbasket of the continent." with its rich agricultural history and diverse landscapes having played a crucial role in shaping not only the nation's economy but also its global standing in the agricultural sector.

Economic and political instability have, at times, cast shadows over the agricultural landscape. These challenges have had a profound impact on the once-thriving sector, requiring resilience and innovation to navigate building visionary industries that transforms the nation and those around it.

The revival of the agricultural sector through innovations, technology and political will is evident across the continent. We continue to witness a determined effort to revive its agricultural sector through the infusion of modern technology as a pivotal element in transforming traditional farming practices as well as supporting animal conservation initiatives for multiplication, to cultivate the opportunity to transform lives

The Digital Revolution and EdTech

Most exciting, probably, are the prospects held by EdTech, as someone that was educated in the continent through high school. I believe that AI and the technological revolution present so much potential to the young population of Africa at all levels with the availability of Core free education for all. With a young and growing population, there is a need to provide quality education and training to equip individuals with the skills they need to thrive in the modern workforce.

Online education platforms are becoming more popular, making it easier for people to access quality education from anywhere in the world, meaning that access could soon be not just limited to the few but connected to all.

Professional development programs are another area where technology is enabling the acceleration of education and skills development. The Pan African University is a specific intentional initiative within Agenda 2063 that helps drive this initiative.

Offset requirements in Africa

This may not be something that is familiar to you however, I would like to take an example of this as a project within a specific sector that I can relate to that diaspora can engage with for global investment opportunities. This may highlight the pattern and opportunities in each member state within the continent. Within the technology sector, there may be offsetting requirements that can support business growth within the continent.

The offset requirements for a country, often referred to as "offset agreements" or "industrial participation programs," are policies or regulations established by a government to ensure that foreign companies or contractors involved in defence and aerospace contracts contribute to the country's economy in specific ways.

These requirements are typically applied in the context of defence procurement and government contracts. The specifics of offset requirements can vary from one country to another, and they are usually negotiated as part of defence or aerospace contracts. Some common aspects of offset requirements include:

Investment: Foreign companies or contractors may be required to make investments in the host country's economy. This could involve setting up manufacturing facilities, research and development centres, or other types of infrastructure.

Technology Transfer: There may be a stipulation that requires the transfer of technology or technical knowledge to local companies. This is often done to enhance the host country's industrial capabilities.

Local Sourcing: Offset agreements may include commitments to source a certain percentage of materials, components, or services locally. This can help stimulate the local industries and create jobs.

Training and Education: Companies may be required to invest in workforce development and training programs to enhance the skills of the local workforce.

Export Promotion: Some offset agreements might encourage local companies to export their products or services by providing support or incentives.

Countertrade: In some cases, offset agreements can involve countertrade, where foreign companies are required to buy local goods or services as part of the agreement.

Timeframes: Offset requirements often have specific timeframes within which these obligations must be fulfilled. These timeframes can vary depending on the contract and the country's regulations.

A short story that may illustrate this point; Rwanda has always been part of my story within the context of this book so I will again share one from here. I am reminded of an occasion on which I visited Rwanda a few years after the conference I mentioned at the beginning of this book.

With opportunity in hand of executing on my will to understand the mutual benefits and opportunities. I made this trip with a global representative of one of the world's largest aviation companies. This to me was a moment of great fulfilment, because for several years previously, I had diligently worked to understand how we could find mutual benefit for united prosperity between this company and the countries across the continent.

This was a particular opportunity that I believed provided the right backdrop both in terms of security and opportunity. During the flight to Kigali, I was looking through some of the readings I had been doing, and one of the documents I came across was the foundation of the meeting that I planned to achieve some alignment to find mutually beneficial opportunities between the ambitions of the company and the department of transport.

I excitedly sent this off to my colleague with great anticipation of what could come out of a conversation on these subjects. Upon meeting with my colleague, we aligned on the priorities for our representation for a series of meetings with Rwandan government officials.

These meetings were very successful, and our efforts were crowned when we were granted an audience with the Minister of Transport for Rwanda. Unfortunately, my colleague was unable to be present at this final meeting, and being the person responsible for the plan, I had to step into the meeting on his behalf. The formalities of the meeting and my sincere inexperience had me nervous, however, my conviction and willingness to share put me in the room with the Minister of Transport and her high-level delegates in the country.

This was an honour for me, but I felt that my output at the meeting could have been better if I had prepared better. Right after, I called one of my mentors who allayed all my worries. I was greatly relieved, but even more than that, determined to commit to be prepared in future to speak about what I believe in.

I cited this example to illustrate that opportunities exist, and that you should be open to and prepared for them.

When looking at the topic of offset, there are a few countries in the continent that come to mind. This I believe is still a relatively new concept constantly evolving in its reach and opportunity.

However, this provides opportunity for both joint prosperity and a global competitive advantage to both the host nation and the company which would like access to the market.

This win-win situation is something that I would dare the diaspora to look into within their own home countries and launch similar initiatives in their industries to allow for a competitive edge in this ever-dynamic global marketplace in which companies need to compete. Africa has the resources, people and opportunities to compete on a global stage. This will not only open opportunities for international companies with which they work but also for the continent in order to foster ambition and growth.

Chapter 10

Financial Services

This is an exciting narrative in the African continent due to the variation of currencies, the value of currencies and the severe lack of correlation with the continental wealth in terms of natural resources. Having lived through the financial crash in Zimbabwe and seeing how financial instability affects every part of society makes me believe in hope for a transformative financial service that empowers both the country and people in a way that provides connected stability.

Financial services have always been a western institution in many cases built on the wealth of African polities and evident in symbols on currencies, the bank of England for example has an ongoing museum project which helps to educate us on this history but also find opportunities to understand and support projects using traditional systems.

Alongside this and despite this historic reliance on these financing methods that come with issues with regards to history and centralisation. Today, Africa, like the world at large, looks toward a means of exchange that can ease the flow and complexities that arise from currency exchanges and fluctuations that thereby ease trade and unite the continent.

In recent years, various financial services have been developed to cater to a wider range of people, including those who were previously excluded from traditional banking systems. Microfinance, for instance, has become a popular alternative to traditional banking, providing small loans and other financial services to low-income individuals and households. Fintech solutions are also gaining traction, offering innovative financial products and services that leverage technology to enhance convenience, accessibility, and affordability.

Likewise, digital banking services and mobile payment systems have revolutionised the financial landscape, allowing people to transact and access financial services using their mobile phones or other digital devices. This has proven particularly beneficial in remote areas, where traditional banking services are often scarce. By harnessing the power of technology, financial institutions have been trialling and bridging the gap between the unbanked and the formal financial system, enabling more people to participate in the economy and reap the benefits of financial inclusion.

Mobile money services like M-Pesa in Kenya and various fintech innovations across the continent have significantly contributed to the ease and security of online payments. In 2019, the value of mobile money transactions in sub-Saharan Africa was estimated at over $456 billion, reflecting a growing digital financial ecosystem.

With the increasing demand for online shopping, e-commerce and the increased access this has become a significant force in the retail industry, which will support the flow of goods across the world's largest free trade area. People are now more comfortable with making purchases online, and this trend is expected to continue in the coming years.

As a result, businesses are looking for ways to enhance their online presence and provide a seamless shopping experience to their customers.

Online marketplaces have emerged as a prime success in Africa's e-commerce landscape. Jumia, often dubbed the 'Amazon of Africa,' operates in multiple countries and offers a diverse range of products, showcasing the potential of online marketplaces. Another notable example is Konga, a Nigerian e-commerce platform that has gained traction by providing a variety of goods to a wide customer base.

The rise of digital payment solutions has been a game-changer, addressing a critical need for secure transactions in online shopping.

In 2019, the value of mobile money transactions in sub-Saharan Africa was estimated at over $456 billion, reflecting a growing digital financial ecosystem.

Logistics and fulfilment services are also essential components of the e-commerce ecosystem.

Efficient and reliable logistics services are necessary for the timely delivery of products, while fulfilment services ensure that orders are processed and shipped out quickly and accurately.

Within the e-commerce ecosystem, logistics and fulfilment services play a pivotal role. Companies like DHL eCommerce Africa and Aramex are enhancing the efficiency of delivery services. DHL eCommerce Africa has introduced nationwide delivery in several African countries, showcasing the continent's commitment to reliable logistics.

In today's fast-paced and ever-changing business landscape, companies must adapt to new technologies to stay competitive. Digital services and software development have become critical aspects of modern business operations, enabling companies to streamline processes, improve efficiency, and enhance customer experiences.

In order to excel in these areas, companies must invest in the right tools and expertise. This might mean hiring professionals with specialised skills like *cybersecurity experts, data analysts, or digital marketing strategists*.

Additionally, businesses must stay up-to-date with the latest technologies and best practices to ensure they remain competitive and secure in the digital landscape.

These innovations are heralding a profound shift in how individuals across Africa interact with money and financial institutions, embodying the principles of accessibility, efficiency, and inclusivity.

Digital payments have emerged as a transformative force, enabling swift and hassle-free transactions without the need for physical cash or cards. Mobile banking has further amplified accessibility, allowing individuals to manage their finances seamlessly while on the move, aligning with the dynamic and mobile-driven landscape of Africa.

A noteworthy facet of this fintech evolution is peer-to-peer lending, offering a lifeline to those previously excluded from traditional banking systems. This avenue provides opportunities for individuals, *especially entrepreneurs*, to secure funding for their ventures, driving economic growth and fostering a ***culture of entrepreneurship***.

Blockchain technology, with its enhanced security and transparency, is reshaping the financial sector. It has the potential to revolutionise the way financial institutions conduct transactions, track assets, and verify identities, aligning with the call for secure and reliable financial infrastructure in *The Africa We Want*.

Robo-advisory, which is the ability to leverage sophisticated algorithms, is democratising investment opportunities by providing automated and cost-effective investment advice. This empowers individuals to make informed non-bias-based decisions and manage their portfolios efficiently, advancing financial literacy and availability of investment across the continent.

These algorithms are designed to optimise asset allocation and investment strategies based on individual goals and preferences. Primarily the benefits of robo-advisory include accessibility, lower costs, and the ability to implement disciplined and data-driven investment strategies.

This may not be the best method for all levels but what it does do is provide the opportunity to reach all people in all cultures with the same foundational level of opportunity.

In the realm of insurtech, disruptive technologies like telematics and artificial intelligence are redefining insurance dynamics. Insurance companies can now offer personalised and tailor-made policies based on individual risk profiles, optimising coverage and ensuring inclusivity within the insurance landscape.

As the continent advances towards *the Africa We Want*, embracing and uniting fintech innovations will support in driving the African agenda forward. These opportunities present a myriad of local, continental and global markets for Africa and its Diaspora. I believe that we are the generation that not only sees but believes that this is possible. With the right resources and knowledge and global footprint, Africa can harness the power of digital services to drive growth, innovation, and success.

What are you, O great mountain [of obstacles]? Before Zerubbabel, you will become a plain!
-Zechariah son of Iddo, c.520 BCE

Chapter 11

Environment And Development

The Inga dam project is an archetype of Africa's commitment to becoming the green continent, leading the charge against climate change. In a world grappling with the pressing challenges of climate change, the necessity for renewable energy and clean technologies has never been more pronounced. Governments globally are setting ambitious targets to slash carbon emissions, highlighting the urgent need to transition towards sustainable energy sources.

Africa is emerging as a frontrunner in the adoption of renewable energy sources. Solar power, wind power, hydro power, and geothermal power exemplify the continent's dedication to eco-friendliness and sustainability. Not only are these sources environmentally sustainable, but their increasing affordability and efficiency are democratising access to sustainable energy for businesses and individuals alike.

Moreover, there has been remarkable innovation in the realm of energy storage, a pivotal aspect of Africa's green vision. Energy storage technologies, such as advanced batteries and capacitors, are rapidly advancing in terms of both sophistication and cost-effectiveness. This advancement is enabling the reliable and efficient use of renewable energy sources, bolstering Africa's journey towards a sustainable energy landscape.

Smart grid technologies are another pivotal area of growth within the renewable energy sector. These technologies optimise the distribution of energy, ensuring efficient delivery to areas of utmost need while significantly reducing energy wastage. This aligns with Africa's vision of an energy-efficient future, where every unit of energy is utilised judiciously.

Energy efficiency solutions are gaining prominence, and are key as we move forward to a greener planet as both governments and businesses strive to curtail energy consumption. Africa is embracing energy-efficient technologies such as LED lighting and smart thermostats as well as manual powered lighting systems underscoring a commitment to reduce energy usage and mitigate costs, a fundamental principle of Africa Agenda 2063.

The burgeoning field of biotechnology is emerging as a key enabler of the continent's vision for a prosperous and sustainable future. Biotechnology encompasses the use of living organisms, cells, and biological systems to develop and create useful products and technologies. It harnesses the natural processes of living things to solve problems, make new products, or improve existing ones. Understanding the natural ecosystem to harness its patterns for another, this wide-ranging discipline includes genetic engineering, biopharmaceuticals, and agricultural biotechnology, all of which align with Agenda 2063's goals of harnessing innovation for societal advancement.

The advancements in technology and research within the biotechnology sector are expected to propel substantial growth. This growth, in turn, will present new and unprecedented opportunities for innovation and investment, aligning perfectly with the ethos of Agenda 2063. The potential of biotechnology to revolutionise various sectors, including healthcare, agriculture, and industry, is a testament to its significance in shaping Africa's future but our ability to take action on these initiatives is what will enable this to be seen and achieved sooner.

Human capital development is expanding and there will be a growing demand for skilled professionals proficient in areas such as data analytics, software development, and medical research. Investing in education and training in these fields will empower the African workforce to actively participate in the burgeoning industries to lead infrastructure and development by fostering innovation and ensuring Africa remains competitive on the global stage.

In essence, the rise of biotechnology in alignment with Africa's Agenda 2063 showcases the continent's proactive stance in harnessing cutting-edge advancements for the collective benefit of its people.

The growing emphasis on sustainability and conscious consumerism has led to increased demand for sustainable and plant-based products. This includes areas such as renewable packaging, eco-friendly products, organic and natural food, plant-based alternatives, and ethical fashion. Africa as a continent of untapped sustainable products and traditional material that rivals and stands unique from any other is potentially an industry poised to explode with its diaspora looking for Pan-African branding.

As consumers have become more aware of the impact their choices have on the environment, they are looking for products that align with their values. Sustainable and plant-based products have become a popular choice for those who want to reduce their carbon footprint and support ethical practices.

In the core of our human creativity and ability to solve problems and in this lies an untapped treasure trove - sustainable and plant-based products, are a testament to the unique expanse of the continent's rich heritage and unique offerings. There is opportunity for Pan-African brands to rise and embrace this burgeoning industry, fuelled by a growing global consciousness towards sustainability and ethical choices.

Consumers, more than ever, seek products that align with their values, products that transcend mere transactions and resonate with a deeper purpose. Sustainable and plant-based products have emerged as the result of this transformative shift, answering the call to reduce carbon footprints and support ethical practices.

Renewable packaging is one such solution that stands as a vanguard in this movement, offering alternatives to single-use plastics and meeting a dire need for responsible packaging solutions. Simultaneously, eco-friendly products like reusable bags, straws, and water bottles are weaving a fabric of change, gaining traction among conscious consumers. This is not only a continental issue and opportunity but a global one that the continent and diaspora is well placed to support.

In the realm of nourishment, the demand for organic and natural foods is surging, an anthem against harmful chemicals and additives. Plant-based alternatives, from meat substitutes to dairy-free options, are asserting their presence, catering to those embracing a lifestyle with reduced reliance on animal products. With the AfCFTA (African Continental Free Trade Area) and developments in agriculture, this is another opportunity to use local expertise and global knowledge to create a global impact.

Fashion, too, embraces this sustainability revolution. Ethical fashion, rooted in fair labour and sustainable materials, is witnessing a rise in demand as consumers strive to wear their values. African countries produce some of the most beautiful intricately designed materials that are already today used by global well-known high-end brands.

Local fashion designers are tailoring clothes with quality materials that have sustainable and local impact. As the diaspora leads in embracing African designs in place of westernised wear, we can create demand which drives employment, opportunities and pride for African design and brands to not only change the narrative but increase the affluence of these well produced materials that align with the global ambitions to be more sustainable.

Taking this further, fashion is an expression of something more than mere fabric; it's a narrative woven from the threads of history, tradition, and aspiration. The African continent, a mosaic of cultures, each with its unique style, is a fertile ground for fashion that speaks to the soul. From the intricate patterns of West Africa to the bold prints of East Africa, from the flowing garments of North Africa to the vibrant hues of the South, every stitch narrates a story of identity and pride.

In this I imagine the ability for us to create through these patterns, a vibrant canvas of culture, heritage, and creativity, with a brand that mirrors the collective spirit of the African Union. A brand that stands tall and proud, showcasing Africa's diverse tapestry and Pan-African essence.

So as you imagine a brand that effortlessly marries these diverse styles, transcending geographical boundaries and celebrating the unity that underpins the African spirit, this in itself holds a fashion revolution that whispers of collective identity and embraces the unique beauty that each culture brings to the table. It's a runway where diversity takes the spotlight, and unity walks hand in hand with creativity.

Such a brand isn't just a fashion statement; it's a movement. A movement that not only reshapes wardrobes but also reshapes minds. It redefines how the world perceives Africa and how Africa embraces itself. It unites the diaspora, the sons and daughters of Africa scattered across the globe, under the same flag of Pan-African pride.

Chapter 12

Artificial Intelligence And Automation

The advancement of artificial intelligence (AI) and automation technologies is reshaping industries across sectors. Opportunities exist in areas such as AI-powered applications, robotics, autonomous vehicles, machine learning, and process automation.

As these technologies continue to improve and become more widespread, they are transforming the way businesses operate and how work is done. AI-powered applications can help companies streamline processes, analyse data more effectively, and improve customer experiences.

Statistics tell a tale of seismic change. AI-powered applications, for instance, have surged in adoption, with over 60% of companies integrating AI into their operations, according to a 2021 PwC survey. This transformation is not mere conjecture; it's a vivid reality etched in data.

Robotics and autonomous vehicles have the potential to revolutionise manufacturing and transportation industries, making processes faster, cheaper, and more efficient. Machine learning is enabling businesses to make more accurate predictions and better decisions based on data analysis. Process automation is reducing the need for human intervention in repetitive tasks, freeing up employees to focus on more creative and strategic work.

Across the stage, we witness a captivating performance of AI-powered applications, robotics, autonomous vehicles, machine learning, and process automation. Each, a virtuoso in its own right, contributing to a harmonious symphony of innovation that is poised to support and empower the generation that dares to engage and drive it forward.

Robotics and autonomous vehicles have the potential to transform various sectors that touch many facets of life; this includes manufacturing and transportation, orchestrating movements that are faster, leaner, and infinitely precise. Research by the World Economic Forum suggests that by 2025, (Only two years from now!) automation and AI may displace 85 million jobs but also create 97 million new ones, emphasising the need for workforce adaptation. This simply means that there is an opportunity for re-education and as there will not only be more jobs available but new opportunities for enterprise and entrepreneurship.

Education is not a way to escape poverty, it is a way of fighting it. – Julius Nyerere

---

Yet, there is an element that as this grand performance unfolds, a subplot of concern emerges — the fear of job displacement and the ethical dimensions of wielding such unprecedented power. Companies, as vigilant custodians of progress, must guide their workforces through this evolution, ensuring they are not left behind in this revolution of change.

Reskilling and upskilling initiatives are the notes that empower the workforce to keep pace with this dynamic melody. The charge is not just to re-educate but to reach in deeper and locate your core in order to happily let go of some of the tasks AI can do and bring to it human intelligence and creativity which is something I believe it will never be able to do as a human does simply because we live.

Education is a relay for transformative Technology (EdTech)that is poised to open opportunities of understanding to many that have not until now had the opportunity. This is something that excites me at my core as this progress resounds with opportunities such as: e-learning platforms, online tutoring, educational content development, and the promising realms of virtual reality (VR) and augmented reality (AR).

The ***availability of this technology*** is instrumental in the momentum that the diaspora can play in moving the continent ahead in terms of understanding the global dynamic, opportunities and tailoring these to the specificities of the continent to ensure alignment with the local needs and opportunities for entrepreneurship to meet agenda 2063's initiative for the 1M next level.

"During the Forum H.E. Moussa Faki Mahamat, the Chairperson of the AUC launched the 1 Million Next Level Initiative where he encouraged all stakeholders including government, civil society, youth and private and public sector partners to support

the implementation of the initiative which seeks to provide opportunities for ***300 million African youth by 2030*** *in the areas of Education, Employment, Entrepreneurship, Engagement as well as Health & Wellbeing."*

As well as addressing this in an accelerated manner which can address the brain drain challenge that has been faced by the migration of people across the world.

Simply put, AI-powered applications stand ready to unleash their potential, enhancing our world with unprecedented efficiency and allowing a leapfrog for Africa.

I believe that we are part of that generation that is called to unite and understand that it is our joint movement that brings with it an unstoppable force and light. To light the continent with understanding, and empower every sector through character development, role models, mentoring, reverse mentoring and knowledge sharing.

Chapter 13

Smart Cities, Urban Solutions and Rural Preservation?

Imagine cities meticulously designed and powered by cutting-edge technology, where connectivity and efficiency intertwine seamlessly. These smart cities serve as epicentres of innovation, propelling economic prosperity while preserving the environment. As Africa embraces this technological leap, it not only elevates its own communities but also sends ripples across the world.

At the same time the conservation of rural communities and cultures presents an interesting narrative in the tapestry of progress. Smart cities serve as the loom, weaving together vital components. Renewable energy sources and efficient waste management systems form the warp and weft, creating a sustainable infrastructure. Transportation networks, powered by AI and IoT, thread through, enabling smooth and intelligent mobility. Data analytics and smart governance act as the guiding hands, ensuring a holistic and responsive urban experience.

The fabric woven by these cities is not confined to the African continent; it extends its reach globally into the diaspora, connecting the diaspora seamlessly to the continent through solutions which are crafted to address unique African challenges.

Indeed, smart cities in Africa are not just urban centres; they are catalysts for a world that yearns for sustainability, efficiency, and progress. Through them, we can redefine what is possible, creating a future where the interconnectedness of nations, technologies, and ideas transforms the world into a unified powerhouse, where each thread contributes to the strength and beauty of the whole.

This is a vision not just for Africa but for the global African community to connect back to the continent and create the demand that develops growth and opportunity throughout the continent.

"A wise person will always find a way." - African Proverb

The internet has facilitated the rise of remote work and freelancing which presents unique opportunities for people in rural communities to interact with people across the globe. The magnitude of change which could potentially be brought to a single community through the internet could be supported by willing unified actions in line with the local needs and ambitions, thus facilitating the expansion of the ecosystem while minimising adverse effects on nature and villages, and instead, promoting their well-being through connecting them strategically.

This approach aims to foster ecosystem growth in a manner that minimises its impact for long term sustainability. Moreover, it actively supports and contributes to the well-being of these natural environments and communities.

Online platforms and communication tools also enable individuals to work for companies or clients located anywhere in the world, providing greater flexibility and access to a global job market. This has expanded employment opportunities, especially for knowledge-based and digital work. Remote work and freelancing have emerged as dynamic solutions, revolutionising the global job market and redefining employment paradigms.

In the digital age, geographical borders are fading away, and a new era of work is dawning upon us. This transformation is powered by the internet, allowing professionals to transcend the constraints of traditional office setups and connect globally. This call is to do so through your roots in the mother continent.

Taking a data based view of this the statistics speak for themselves. According to a report by FlexJobs, between 2005 and 2017, there was a 159% increase in remote work. In the United States alone, 4.3 million employees (3.2% of the workforce) now work from home at least half the time. This trend is mirrored globally, with countries across the world seeing a surge in remote work adoption.

Africa, with its burgeoning digital infrastructure and a diaspora spanning the globe, stands on the precipice of a profound opportunity. By aligning with the global trend of remote work and freelancing, Africa can leverage the skills, expertise, and influence of its diaspora to penetrate international markets.

For instance, African freelancers, equipped with strong digital skills, are increasingly sought after in the global economy.

Platforms like Upwork and Fiverr have provided a stage for African talent to offer services ranging from digital marketing to software development to a vast global clientele. This, in turn, creates a channel for revenue flow into the continent, supporting economic growth and sustainability. The intentionality to empower Africans through these means is in the hands of us all.

By tapping into the potential of remote work and freelancing, Africa can at the same time address its brain drain challenge. Skilled professionals from the African Diaspora can contribute to the continent's development by working on projects, providing expertise, and investing in local initiatives, all facilitated through the digital realm.

The world at large has the talent and the tools; it's time to embrace the global stage and realise the vision of a connected and empowered continent.

Finally, entrepreneurship education is also becoming more important in Africa. With a growing number of startups and small businesses, there is a need to provide education and training to help entrepreneurs succeed. By providing access to resources and support, aspiring entrepreneurs can learn how to start and grow successful businesses, which can in turn contribute to economic growth and job creation.

Chapter 14

Sustainability Of Our Beautiful Continent

Africa is the most beautiful place I have had the privilege to travel to and live in. There is a grounding and connection like no other, I am personally looking forward to visiting every single member state in the continent as the ease of travel allows for more access through Agenda 2063.

AU - Aspiration 1: *A prosperous Africa based on inclusive growth and sustainable development.*

Many countries in Africa have a unique quality; the seamless blend of urban development and its characteristic bustle, with the serene scenes of nature. Agenda 2063 for this reason places a strong emphasis on sustainability and envisions a prosperous and sustainable Africa. The agenda recognizes the need for Africa to ***develop in a manner that is socially, economically, and environmentally sustainable***.

In Africa we have the unique opportunity to build correctly from the beginning. We are in an age of technology that allows the ability to bypass most of the outdated technology in existence and advance to the more sustainable and environmentally friendly solutions. This is a call to drive the development of these technologies to meet the unique needs of the continent in order to create a plan of action.

Sustainable Development Goals (SDGs): Agenda 2063 aligns with the United Nations Sustainable Development Goals. This supports the global picture which connects the Diaspora to opportunities to utilise the strategic framework to support opportunities for development across the continent. In the references of this book you will find a link to a table that clearly identifies the African Unions SDGs and the correlation to the UN's SDGs.

"Knowledge is a garden. If it isn't cultivated, you can't harvest it."

Similar to the global picture on this subject there are many opportunities for innovative solutions and ideas. Understanding how to connect these back to the continent first comes with understanding of the local issues. Agenda 2063 recognises this and points to a few key areas of potential areas of collaboration and development. Let us look at some of these opportunities at a high level.

This shift towards renewable energy is a crucial step in achieving Agenda 2063's vision of a prosperous, integrated, and united Africa. By adopting clean energy solutions, African countries can reduce their dependence on fossil fuels, which are not only finite but also contribute significantly to climate change. In addition to mitigating the effects of global warming, renewable energy can also provide access to affordable and reliable energy for millions of people who currently live without it. This, in turn, can spur economic growth, create jobs, and improve the standard of living across the continent. With the right investments and policies in place, Africa can lead the way in the global transition to a sustainable, low-carbon future.

One of the key factors that make Africa vulnerable to climate change impacts is its heavy reliance on rain-fed agriculture. Climate change can lead to unpredictable rainfall patterns, droughts, and floods, which can significantly reduce crop yields and threaten food security. To address this challenge, Agenda 2063 calls for the promotion of sustainable agriculture practices, such as conservation agriculture and agroforestry, which can help to improve soil health, retain moisture, and increase crop yields.

Healthy ecosystems can also act as natural buffers against climate change impacts, such as floods and landslides. To this end, the agenda calls for the conservation and restoration of forests, wetlands, and other critical ecosystems.

Strengthening the continent through disaster preparedness and response capacities in Africa is key with such a vast landmass in a continent. Climate change is expected to increase the frequency and intensity of extreme weather events, such as storms, floods, and heatwaves, which can cause significant damage and loss of life. As we learn from the global occurrences and leverage opportunity we can mitigate these risks quicker.

Strategic actions are being executed to ensure Africa's development in a way that is socially, economically, and environmentally sustainable. This means that African countries work together to ensure that the use of natural resources does not lead to irreversible damage to ecosystems and the depletion of natural resources.

Mechanisms are being implemented that ensure transparency, accountability, and participation of all stakeholders in decision-making processes related to natural resource management. This includes the involvement of local communities, civil society organisations, and the private sector in the development of policies and strategies that promote responsible and sustainable natural resource management.

Furthermore, Agenda 2063 recognizes the importance of conserving biodiversity and protecting ecosystems to ensure their resilience and sustainability. This requires the adoption of integrated approaches that balance conservation and development objectives, using tools such as ecosystem-based management, sustainable land use planning, and biodiversity conservation.

The African Union recognizes the significant role that agriculture plays in the continent's economic development and growth. This is something that we looked at earlier in the book that connects to many goals and ambitions of which sustainable agriculture practices is one of them not only to ensure food security, but also contribute to the reduction of poverty, creation of employment opportunities, and improvement of rural livelihoods.

Investment in agricultural research and innovation is necessary to improve agricultural productivity, develop drought-resistant crops, and enhance soil fertility. Furthermore, promoting agroecology, which is the application of ecological principles to agriculture, can help reduce the use of harmful pesticides and fertilisers, protect biodiversity, and enhance soil health.

Finally, support for smallholder farmers is vital to ensure that they have access to the necessary resources, such as land, credit, and agricultural inputs, to enhance their productivity and improve their livelihoods. By prioritising sustainable agriculture and food security, Africa can achieve its development goals and build a prosperous future for its citizens.

Access to quality education and skills development in rural areas aims to ensure that rural communities have access to formal and informal education and training opportunities. This enables individuals in rural areas to acquire relevant skills, knowledge, and competencies for employment, entrepreneurship, and overall human development.

There is much untapped potential especially with regard to the rural women and youth as agents of change and development. In light of this, Agenda 2063 promotes gender equality, women's empowerment, and youth inclusion in rural development initiatives. This involves creating opportunities for women and youth to access education, economic resources, leadership roles, and participation in decision-making processes.

This is something that I am passionately involved in within the STEM industries as this is a global issue with initiatives such as Paradigm for parity, 2030 and Youth 2030: The United Nations Youth Strategy some of the projects that are leading the charge globally. On a local level AWAYA (Women and youth in Aviation) are working diligently to understand how we unite on these initiatives.

> *UN Youth Strategy: "The strategy has five priority areas: youth engagement, participation and advocacy; ensuring informed and healthy foundations through education and health care; economic empowerment through decent work; human rights; and peace and resilience building.*

Community participation and inclusive governance in rural development processes is an essential part of the development. It emphasises the importance of involving local communities in decision-making, planning, and implementation of development programs. This ensures that rural communities have a voice and are *actively engaged* in shaping their own development trajectories.

By focusing on these specific actions, Agenda 2063 seeks to strategically target and create an enabling environment that unlocks the potential yet keeps the beauty of rural areas, it aims to improve livelihoods, reduce inequalities, and foster sustainable development in rural communities across Africa as an important part of the picture.

An example of this implementation is how the South African government now officially recognises the different regional tribes releasing the entrenched social and economic effects.

Chapter 15

Will You Activate Your Call?

Agenda 2063 is a visionary and ambitious plan for the development of Africa over the next 50 years. It aims to transform the continent into a prosperous, peaceful, and integrated entity, driven by its own citizens and representing a dynamic force in the global arena.

The agenda identifies key priority areas such as agriculture, infrastructure, education, health, science and technology, and gender equality, among others.

When we come to the realisation that there is ***enough*** *for everyone to be truly fulfilled and live in a way that shows that. There will be.*

It also emphasises the need for greater regional integration and unity, as well as the promotion of good governance, democracy, and human rights. To achieve these objectives, Agenda 2063 requires the active participation and engagement of all Africans, including civil society, the private sector, and the youth.

By staying informed and educated about Agenda 2063, you can contribute to this historic effort to shape the future of Africa and create a better world for all.

I learned that courage was not the absence of fear, but the triumph over it. The brave man is not he who does not feel afraid, but he who conquers that fear.
— Nelson Mandela

Getting involved in Agenda 2063 requires active participation and contribution to the realisation of the agenda's objectives. If you have reached the end of this book and you are still not sure where to start. Let down your net, take a step into one of the options you will read next.

Here are some key ways to engage in Agenda 2063:

Stay Informed: Educate yourself about the vision, aspirations, and objectives of Agenda 2063. Familiarise yourself with the priority areas and sectors identified in the agenda. Stay updated on the progress, policies, and initiatives related to Agenda 2063 at the continental, regional, and national levels.

"Hands wash each other" African Proverb

Being a part of the African Diaspora or an advocate for it is just as important. As a continent, Africa is looking for partners and allies for large scale business ventures, and the diaspora should be more than ready to join this group. This book is not about exclusivity towards African people or her diaspora, but rather about gaining an understanding of the potential of Africa and the ability to develop beyond ourselves and affect change from the continent and into the global arena.

"There is no beauty but the beauty of action"
– African Proverb

Contributing specific skills, knowledge, or expertise relevant to the priority areas of Agenda 2063, plays an important role in developing the African continent which has a youthful population in need of mentorship and guidance. This could involve participating in research, sharing best practices, providing technical assistance, or offering mentorship to individuals and organisations working towards the agenda's objectives.

Persistence in focusing on a single desire.

Engage: If you are part of the African Diaspora, explore opportunities to engage with diaspora-focused initiatives that align with Agenda 2063. Look for organisations, networks, and platforms that facilitate diaspora engagement, such as investment forums, mentorship programs, or cultural exchange initiatives.

Attend conferences, workshops, and events focused on African development to connect with stakeholders and build partnerships. Engage in cross-sectoral collaborations to foster innovation and maximise impact.

Get involved in local initiatives and projects that contribute to the objectives of Agenda 2063. Volunteer your time and skills with organisations working on issues such as education, healthcare, environmental conservation, entrepreneurship, and community development.

"For many years I have wanted so deeply to belong to be accepted as I am. When I found this belonging was inside, in my willingness to be true to me, I found it outside."

Engaging at the grassroots level can make a tangible difference and contribute to the overall vision of Agenda 2063.

"The majority of the world's 1.8 billion young people live in developing countries, and their numbers are expected to continue growing."

Consider supporting sustainable businesses and investments in Africa. This could involve investing in African enterprises, supporting local entrepreneurs, or purchasing products and services that promote sustainable practices, social inclusion, and environmental stewardship.

"As an entrepreneur, don't just build a business; build an institution that will outlast you."
–Strive Masiyiwa (Econet Wireless)

Engage with Policy Processes and stay informed about policy developments related to Agenda 2063 at the national and regional levels. Engage with policymakers, participate in public consultations, and provide input to shape policies that align with the agenda's objectives. Advocate for policy coherence and implementation of Agenda 2063 in national development plans.

When meditating on how to complete this book–and what in many ways feels like a chapter in my story or journey to see and empower the vision for the African continent, I came across a book that engrossed my imagination not only of what could be but of what is.

Whilst walking to get some food one day with my son in London, I saw a shop with a small section of second-hand books. I for one love old books for many reasons, one of them being the depth in the books. I also enjoy seeing the inscriptions they might have that intrigue me, but more interestingly, they leave a true “sold” sign which means that someone at sometime saw this as inspiration in the local area.

"An army of sheep led by a lion can defeat an army of lions led by a sheep."

As I scanned the shelf, one of the books caught my eye. Its title was “A Thousand Hills”. When I looked closer at the subtitle, it read: “Rwanda’s rebirth and the man who dreamt it.” I was blown away by the fact that at this random shop in London, while thinking of the end of this book, I would be met with the story of a leader who inspired the beginning of mine.

This book in many ways has the inspiration of the African people running through it both as personal experiences but also as quotes and guides left by those that led and loved this continent before us.

I wanted to share some insights from the book which I hope in closing will inspire us all and together to begin to see ourselves as one as Rwanda has done, and quoting from Black Panther, one of my favourite Marvel Movies “We need to all learn to live together as if we were one big tribe”.

The conflict and yet beauty in this is not that they tried to make all the tribes one, but rather that they were torn apart by their differences which they eventually began to realise was something that should be celebrated as each tribe’s uniqueness and strengths. In so doing, they found that they fit together seamlessly into a powerful force where each was able to thrive in their space.

I believe that just as Rwanda has turned around their country and imparted to their people a sense of pride and a spirit of excellence, this can be the case for the African people and the diaspora the world over.

Rwanda, a small landlocked country in East Africa, has been on an extraordinary journey of transformation over the past few decades. From a nation scarred by a tragic history of genocide to a shining example of progress and development, Rwanda's turnaround is nothing short of remarkable.

To truly appreciate Rwanda's transformation, we must first understand its historical context. The nation was torn apart by a brutal genocide in 1994, resulting in the loss of hundreds of thousands of lives and widespread destruction. The scars of this dark period were deep, but Rwanda was determined to heal and rebuild.

A critical factor in Rwanda's turnaround has been visionary leadership. President Paul Kagame, who assumed office in 2000, has played a pivotal role in steering the nation towards progress. His leadership style, characterised by accountability and a commitment to development, has been instrumental.

Rwanda has implemented a series of *strategic initiatives* as well as been a part of the African Union’s visionary implementation of agenda 2063, when we look at what President Paul Kagame has done in his country and then look to the strategy for the African Union and his involvement in this I am excited to see this reality just as Rwanda has but this time not just as an observer but as an activist and a proponent of the change.

"Peace and security are not just aspirations; they are prerequisites for our continent's growth and development. We must work together to ensure that Africa is free from conflicts and can thrive in a stable environment."

Rwanda implemented policies to foster economic growth. These include pro-business policies, ease of doing business reforms, and an emphasis on technology and innovation. As a result, the country has witnessed a steady increase in foreign investments. The aviation sector of Rwanda, for example, is now part owned by Qatar Airways.

This is visible at a national level however the most interesting part was when I once had the privilege of spending the day with an amazing African Queen from Rwanda who is a leader herself within her field. Her stories and of how President Paul Kagame inspired a change of mindset and brought about freedom and unity was truly infectious and highlighted to me how the change started one individual at a time.

What she helped me realise is that the change starts from within, and I took this personally and decided to re-educate myself from within.

"We have the potential to transform Africa's economies through trade and investment. Our goal is to create an Africa that is prosperous, self-reliant, and capable of providing opportunities for its people."

Just like Rwanda has done as a nation, I believe that as individuals as we do this it increases momentum and causes a movement. Although all these opportunities that motivated me on, for someone that loves books never did it occur to me that I would write one myself. So, this in itself is testament not only to our ability to grow, change and use our experience as a light for others but also for ourselves, it is the light within.

About the Author

A Journey of Empowerment, Leadership, and Lasting Impact"

A transformative journey in "Empowering Change." Kimberley Grace Patel, is a seasoned professional in the aerospace industry, who shares her narrative as a powerful testament to unwavering commitment to effecting positive change in both in her professional sphere and the communities close to her heart.

As an avionics expert who has worked for two of the largest aviation companies in the world while maintaining a community work ethic alongside this. Kimberley is currently the EuMEA Liaison for RTX Employee Resource Group, representing the voice of the region and contributing to shaping global strategies for the top employee experiences worldwide. She received nomination to the AWAYA (African Women and Youth in Aviation) board for AFCAC as a notable woman of influence in the African continent. Kimberley's story is a tapestry of empowerment, community engagement, and leadership.

Technology and youth empowerment in STEM education has always been something close to the Author. A mother with a beautiful son, this opened her to opportunities to touch as many lives as possible within the spheres of influence. She understood how the global nature of aviation and the reach of AI and technology could multiply her reach and help her share what she has had the privilege to learn.

Some of the projects undertaken include; "Redefining the future of Africa's Aviation" with schools in Kenya and "Establishing social pillars for sustainable growth" with schools in Ethiopia with AfRAA and Collins Aerospace. Tech Engagement with Girls Fly Africa and Avia Dev.

Alongside this as a passionate advocate for DE&I and as the RTX Black Excellence Network - EuMEA Liaison she held multiple educational talks notably in 2023 with Franck Burno the UKs champion heavy weight boxer to advocate for Mental Health Awareness and support of Black History Month UK.

Kimberley is also passionate about personal projects in Zimbabwe where she was born and personal sponsorship of initiatives such as Color My Space – Ghana 2022: Imagine your Africa, create it in your community and 2023: Empowered to take up space.

Professionally, Kimberley excels in building relationships, executing strategies, and fostering excellence. Her passion lies in sharing knowledge with both inside and outside the continent on how to work sustainably for mutual prosperity, strategically connecting with the opportunity that is right for business and empowering the next generation of leaders.

"Empowered through Excellence" encapsulates the author's journey. Inspired by a vision from a video of a serene beach on the cost of West Africa with the caption "Imagine watching the children play, knowing that we made it". The author, passionately pursued the goal, fueled by confidence in love and a commitment to impactful, positive, and lasting change.
Knowing that it was my confidence in love and my wiliness to make an impactful positive and lasting change for as many as possible on the continent and within the diaspora that would bring this to fruition.

Keeping her favorite African proverb in mind.

"...success is not just about what you achieve in your life; it's about what you inspire others to do" - African Proverb

ACKNOWLEDGMENTS

"We're diamonds in the rough," proclaims the African line. With humility and grace, let your presence be, A beacon of love, for all eyes to see.

The journey I embarked on this year was instrumental and I am so grateful to have been found and challenged to enter into this self-discovery of divine purpose which equates with divine fulfilment in life. Although it is always worth remembering that self-discovery of one's purpose takes a lifetime, I am learning that it is fulfilling when you are able to reach a greater dimension. This is something that my grandmother always said and challenged me on. The idea that she would be in a higher dimension than me if I didn't "Famba na Jesu" and walk in my purpose which would mean she would have to come and visit me in the lower dimension.

She challenged me in the most loving way to strive to go further, love deeper and take the risks. There has been a part of me that has and a part that hasn't and the beauty of endurance and character building is in the knowing that you can reach. It is the art of actioning through intentionally bringing light to areas of darkness.

This is something I am still learning and developing every day. A wise man once showed me it takes faith and belief to trust that the promises will come. As I was able to put myself in a place with people that helped re-educate, challenge me on opportunities and talents. I would therefore like to close this book with a word to some people that have inspired my journey including

My mother Grace and father Vincent who are always there, and ran to my side when I needed reassurance and to know that I was enough, and it was my life and my race to run and chose for myself what I wanted. I love you and am so grateful that I had the opportunity to be inspired by your light.

My family who has been both inspirational but also patient in allowing me time and space to find myself. My sisters (Michelle, Nicole, Tonya Hannah and Lana) family and friends who have supported me especially with Josiah and the dogs I am so grateful for you all.

Bishop Wayne Malcom, the I can community church programs the book on the re-education of the masses and for the timely insights. As well as the Kingdoms University in which I met a community of inspirational people on a journey of greatness.

RTX BXN (RTX Black Excellence Network) and the women in AWAYA (African Women and Youth in Aviation), who are constant supporters and uplifters of each other.

My mentors, colleagues and friends, who have guided me to people who can support. Put in me words of encouragement to push me forward and believed that I could even when I didn't. Including Hannah who has been my constant advocate support and trusting ear.

My girlfriends who have been on the other side of the phone for the longest conversations or there for a long walk in the park I truly treasure you.

Fadimatou Noutchemo, Maureen Khaonge and Daniel Ayree, I am grateful for your inspiration by being the change in your own lives you helped keep me motivated that I could do greater things in mine.

Christian thank you for inviting me into a community, for showing me I could reach back past all the hurt and moving me forward to freedom empowered. For bringing the light that I needed in the darkness by reminding me who I am.

Josiah, my son who has put up with my endless hours of studying and working. With patience and the purest love, I cannot explain how truly grateful I am to have you in my life and how honoured I am to be your mother.

To my father in heaven, I am eternally grateful.

RESOURCES & SOURCES

The AU Commission | African Union

Education, Science, Technology & Innovation (ESTI) | African Union (au.int)

Linking Agenda 2063 and the SDGs | African Union (au.int)

THE 17 GOALS | Sustainable Development (un.org)

Paradigm for Parity - Fighting for Gender Parity (paradigm4parity.org)

UN SG launches #Youth2030 strategy - United Nations Sustainable Development

Ghana's Pan African Heritage Museum seeks to reclaim Africa's history - News

Apartheid - Resistance, Protest, Activism | Britannica

Coins and Colonisation | Bank of England

THE 17 GOALS | Sustainable Development (un.org)

EX CL 1267 XXXVIII_E.pdf (au.int)

Science, Technology and Innovation Strategy for Africa 2024 | African Union (au.int)

Made in the USA
Monee, IL
25 January 2024

75cd2b88-01bf-4b06-b183-2b822b1578d1R01